SIMPLE CONTEMPORARY QUILTS

SIMPLE CONTEMPORARY QUILTS

BOLD NEW DESIGNS FOR THE FIRST-TIME QUILTER

Valerie Van Arsdale Shrader

LARK BOOKS

A Division of Sterling Publishing Co., Inc.
New York

SENIOR EDITOR
Suzanne J.E. Tourtillott

TECHNICAL EDITOR AND WRITER
Peggy Bendel

ART DIRECTOR
Dana Margaret Irwin

COVER DESIGNER
Barbara Zaretsky

ASSOCIATE EDITOR
Nathalie Mornu

ASSOCIATE ART DIRECTOR
Lance E. Wille

ART PRODUCTION ASSISTANT
Jeff Hamilton

EDITORIAL ASSISTANCE
Mark Bloom

EDITORIAL INTERNS
Janet Hurley
Sue Stigleman

ART INTERN
Marshall Hudson

ILLUSTRATOR
Orrin Lundgren

PHOTOGRAPHY
Principal, Stewart O'Shields;
Additional, Paul Jeremias
(page 76)

Library of Congress Cataloging-in-Publication Data

Shrader, Valerie Van Arsdale.
 Simple contemporary quilts : bold new designs for the first-time quilter /
Valerie Van Arsdale Shrader. -- 1st ed.
      p. cm.
 Includes index.
 ISBN-13: 978-1-57990-875-1 (alk. paper)
 ISBN-10: 1-57990-875-6 (alk. paper)
 1. Patchwork. 2. Machine quilting. 3. Appliqué. I. Title.
 TT835.S492 2007
 746.46'041--dc22

                                                      2006100862

10 9 8 7 6 5 4 3 2 1

First Edition

Published by Lark Books, A Division of
Sterling Publishing Co., Inc.
387 Park Avenue South, New York, N.Y. 10016

Text © 2007, Lark Books
Photography © 2007, Lark Books
Illustrations © 2007, Lark Books

Distributed in Canada by Sterling Publishing,
c/o Canadian Manda Group, 165 Dufferin Street
Toronto, Ontario, Canada M6K 3H6

Distributed in the United Kingdom by GMC Distribution Services,
Castle Place, 166 High Street, Lewes, East Sussex, England BN7 1XU

Distributed in Australia by Capricorn Link (Australia) Pty Ltd.,
P.O. Box 704, Windsor, NSW 2756 Australia

The written instructions, photographs, designs, patterns, and projects in this volume
are intended for the personal use of the reader and may be reproduced for that purpose only. Any other use, especially commercial use, is forbidden under law without
written permission of the copyright holder.

Every effort has been made to ensure that all the information in this book is accurate.
However, due to differing conditions, tools, and individual skills, the publisher cannot
be responsible for any injuries, losses, and other damages that may result from the
use of the information in this book.

If you have questions or comments about this book, please contact:
Lark Books
67 Broadway
Asheville, NC 28801
(828) 253-0467

Manufactured in China

ISBN 13: 978-1-57990-875-1
ISBN 10: 1-57990-875-6

For information about custom editions, special sales, premium and corporate pur-
chases, please contact Sterling Special Sales Department at 800-805-5489 or spe-
cialsales@sterlingpub.com.

This book is dedicated
to the new generation
of quilters who will
take textiles, color,
and design in exciting
new directions.

CONTENTS

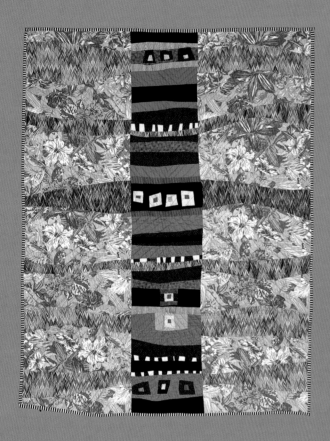

INTRODUCTION 8

BASICS 10

Quilt Materials 10

Basic Tools & Supplies 12

Other Tools & Supplies 14

Planning a Bed Quilt 15

Planning an Art Quilt 16

Essential Machine Sewing Techniques 17

Essential Hand Sewing Techniques . . 21

Essential Quilt Assembly Techniques 22

THE QUILTS 26

Sparrow 28

Flicka 32

The Square Root of Yin and Yang . . . 36

Space Age Lounge 40

Tumbling Leaves 44

Easy Chenille 48

Retro Sashiko 53

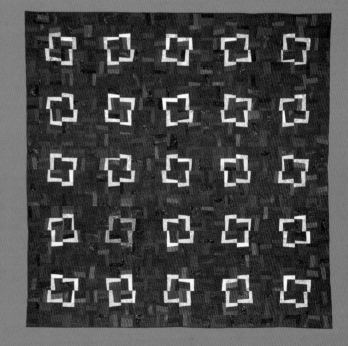

Wild Zebra 56

For Baby 60

Zoe's Deep Blue 66

Martini Dot 72

Dancing Squares 76

Flowers 82

Crop Circles 86

Sea Moods 90

Brocade on Parade 94

Constellations 98

Two Trees 102

Little Hills 106

Bold Chintz 112

TEMPLATES 120

ABOUT THE DESIGNERS 127

ACKNOWLEDGMENTS 128

INDEX 128

Introduction

You probably know that quilting is a craft that dates back for centuries. Although its origins were no doubt humble, being a practical joining of layers of fabric to provide warmth and shelter, it wasn't long before decoration became as important as function. The creativity of the quiltmaker was soon introduced into the mix of fabric and filling, and the composition, piecing, and stitching of the quilt became an art form. Indeed, the quilt served as a blank canvas, to be adorned with intricate stitch patterns and blocks of exquisite fabric. Today, while quilts continue to provide comfort, they also satisfy the need for self-expression, as you'll see in the 20 designs presented here in *Simple Contemporary Quilts*.

If you've longed to learn how to quilt, these striking modern projects will offer you a range of possibilities. While these designs are based on easy-to-learn, traditional quilting techniques, they all offer a fresh look at the craft. While some employ piecing techniques, others rely on large blocks or appliqués that make the creation of the quilt top a quick process—perfect for a beginner. Abstract composition, easy embroidery, carefree raw-edge construction, and novel fabrics lend a current sensibility to these quilts. All of the information you need to get started is included here, including planning the size of your quilt, choosing fabric and materials, hand and machine sewing techniques, and assembly options. Best of all, you don't need any special equipment or an expensive sewing machine to get started.

After you've learned the fundamentals, you can apply your creativity to the basic form. The designers in this book found their muse in many places: the constellations, the sea, geometry, modern art—even a favorite cocktail! Contemporary quiltmaking encourages creativity and spontaneity; add elements to your quilt top until you're satisfied with its look. Experiment with nontraditional quilting fabrics such as wool and silk organza, or include needlework, beads, or appliqué for additional ornamentation. *Simple Contemporary Quilts* features both decorative art quilts and functional quilts, in a variety of sizes, from small wall hang-

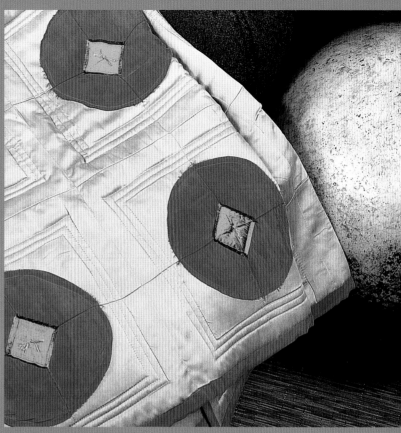

ings to queen-sized bed quilts. The smaller projects are the perfect introduction to quilting, while the larger projects offer you an opportunity to hone your new skills. For a peek into the creative process, see the designers' comments that are sprinkled throughout the first 25 pages.

There's no better time to explore the art of contemporary quiltmaking. With endless choices of fabric and embellishments, you can create functional quilts that are also beautiful pieces of fiber art, with the 20 projects in this book as your inspiration.

BASICS

In *Simple Contemporary Quilts*, creative designers give traditional quilt making methods a modern makeover. The results are the exciting quilts you see on these pages. If you've been interested in quilting, this book, with its emphasis on the latest techniques, will inspire you to try it.

Like quilts from the past, contemporary quilts are made from two layers of fabric with a soft batting in between, but there are exceptions to this rule and to other rules, too. For instance, contemporary quilts have a bold scale. Big blocks and jumbo appliqués give the quilts a fresh sense of style and remarkable visual impact. The bold scale also signifies a whole other way to make quilts. Instead of taking months to cover a quilt top with countless tiny appliqués or precisely pieced blocks, you can complete an entire quilt in a few, short sewing sessions or over the weekend.

Beyond their bold scale and efficient construction, contemporary quilts feature free-form designs that require minimal measuring and marking. Often you have the option of cutting the fabric freehand, arranging the pieces by eye, and quilting along informal stitch paths that meander and flow.

Furthermore, choosing the fabrics that go into a quilt is more adventurous than ever before. While it's perfectly fine to use the plain-weave cotton fabrics quilters have favored for ages, some of the best quilts happen when you venture off the beaten path and use mavericks such as silk shantung, velvet, or lightweight linen. A number of the quilt designs in this book were inspired by novel, sometimes whimsical materials from the bridal and home decorating departments of fabric shops, while others take pieces of vintage textiles and put them to surprising use.

Chances are if you like a fabric, you can make it into a quilt. For example, if the fabric you most adore frays, simply embrace this quality. Turn it into a design feature by letting the raw edges show rather than fighting its nature with old-fashioned seams and turned-under edges. If the fabric is so sheer you can see through it, make the most of its character by using it as an overlay to give an opaque fabric depth and dimension. Relax, have fun, and enjoy the possibilities.

QUILT MATERIALS

Most contemporary quilts consist of two rectangular panels of cloth—the quilt top and the backing—with a soft batting sandwiched in between. These three textile layers are stacked, basted together temporarily, then held together permanently with hand- or machine-quilted stitches (or a combination of both). The raw edges usually are finished with a binding.

The Quilt Top and Backing

The quilt top carries the design. Each project in this book furnishes a list of the fabrics you'll need to duplicate the quilt design that you see in the photograph. If you prefer to use the design as the starting point for an original interpretation, feel free to substitute your choice of materials. You can use the fabric amounts given as a shopping guide, adjusting the estimates accordingly if your selections come in widths other than those listed. For example, if you select a fabric that is narrower in width, you'll need to purchase a greater length of fabric.

The backing is usually plain cloth in a solid color or print that relates to the quilt top's design. If you prefer, this layer can be pieced or embellished to add design interest or to make the quilt reversible. The backing should have the same care requirements as the quilt top.

When the fabrics in a project are prone to shrinkage or have finishes that should be removed prior to sewing, the instructions will direct you to prewash the fabrics as a first step. Otherwise, prewashing is optional. If you choose to prewash the materials for the quilt top, prewash the materials for the quilt backing, too.

The Batting

Loft refers to the thickness of batting. A low-loft batting is suggested for the majority of quilts in this book because most of the designers chose this type. These fairly flat, thin battings are easy to stitch through, and they're not too bulky to maneuver through a typical household sewing machine.

Low-loft battings may be made from pure cotton, cotton/synthetic blends, or all-polyester fibers. Some are needlepunched, glazed, or otherwise processed to make them very stable, and this allows you to quilt as sparingly or as densely as you like. Others are more loosely constructed, are less stable, and require close quilting to prevent the batting from shifting and bunching. Read the batting label to discern the manufacturer's recommendation.

Sign Your Quilt

Like any one-of-a-kind creation, the quilt you sew should be signed. Make a label to sew onto the backing that includes your name, the completion date, and any other information you'd like to record (see figure 1). Write on the label with a permanent fabric marking pen, or use free-motion stitching (see page 19) or programmable embroidery lettering if available on your sewing machine. You can also write directly onto the quilt if you prefer.

Figure 1

At the opposite end of the batting spectrum, there are very puffy, high-loft battings; there are also many battings that belong in between these two extremes. The loftier the batting, the less suitable it is for machine quilting or extensive hand stitching, but the better suited it is for tying by hand (see page 21). A hand-tied quilt made with a high-loft batting will resemble a down-filled comforter and have a luxurious, tufted texture.

Common Batting Sizes

In most cases, the batting should be 4 inches (10.2 cm) longer and wider than the quilt top to provide an allowance for quilting. Many batting brands can be purchased by the yard (meter) in 48-, 90-, 96-, and 124-inch (121.9, 228.6, 243.8, and 315 cm) widths.

Battings also are available packaged in the following precut sizes: craft, 45 x 34 inches (114.3 x 86.4 cm); crib, 60 x 45 inches (152.4 x 114.3 cm); throw, 60 x 60 inches (152.4 x 152.4 cm); twin, 90 x 72 inches (228.6 x 182.9 cm); double/full, 96 x 84 inches (243.8 x 213.4 cm); queen, 108 x 92 inches (274.3 x 233.7 cm); and king, 124 x 120 inches (315 x 304.8 cm). Because the exact measurements of a precut batting vary by brand, read the label to be sure you are purchasing a batting the right size for your needs.

BASIC TOOLS & SUPPLIES

If you have some sewing experience, you probably have most of the gear you'll need to create contemporary quilts. You should have the majority of these items on hand to create any of the projects in this book.

Sewing

A sewing machine that makes a straight and a zigzag stitch is necessary. Newer models may have helpful features such as needle stop up/down, changeable needle positioning, and programmable stitch patterns; these are nice to have but not essential.

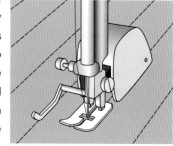

Figure 2

If your model has a built-in even-feed feature that moves the top layer of fabric in harmony with the bottom layer, it will give you an advantage when machine quilting; otherwise, you can purchase an accessory called a walking foot (see figure 2) and attach it to the machine for this purpose. For free motion quilting, you'll need a darning foot (see page 19); usually this accessory is included but it can also be purchased separately. A quilt bar attachment (see page 18) makes it easy to stitch parallel rows without the extra step of marking the quilt; this may be included in the sewing machine's accessory kit or purchased separately.

Most quilts call for a touch of hand sewing, and for this you'll need a needle and thimble. General-purpose needles called sharps in a size from 7 to 11—whatever size you find comfortable—work well. An embroidery needle with a large eye and sharp point will be needed

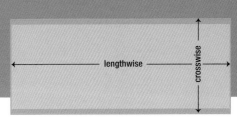

Figure 3

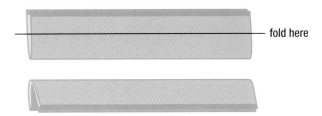

fold here

Figure 4

for quilts that use embroidery floss, perle cotton, or yarn for hand-sewn details.

For basting quilts in the simple contemporary way, you'll need a large quantity of rustproof safety pins. Good, all-purpose choices are pins in the 1- to 2-inch (2.5 to 5.1 cm) size range.

Of course, you'll also need thread. Today there are many kinds of thread available for quilt making. Regular cotton/polyester sewing thread, also called all-purpose thread, works well for the quilts on these pages. This type of thread is widely available in a large selection of colors, so you'll find it easy to purchase what you need for a project. When a quilt design requires a special kind of thread such as monofilament nylon or heavy-duty, the project's materials list will explain what to purchase and the instructions will explain when and how to use it.

Cutting

In addition to common cutting tools such as small scissors and a pair of larger shears, a rotary cutting system saves so much time and effort when making quilts that it belongs in the must-have category. The system requires three tools—the rotary cutter, a clear plastic ruler, and a mat.

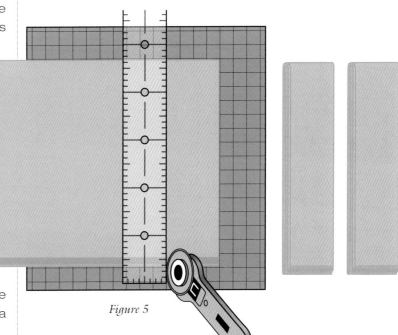

Figure 5

The mat and ruler are printed with a measuring grid calibrated in ¼-inch (6 mm) increments. You can place fabric on the mat, align the ruler and mat grids, and roll the cutting blade along the ruler's edge to measure and cut the fabric with one motion. There's no need to measure or mark the fabric beforehand.

For example, cutting crosswise strips for borders or bindings is a common step when making contemporary quilts, and rotary cutting makes this quick and easy. To begin, understand that "lengthwise" is parallel to the selvages, while "crosswise" is at right angles to the selvages (figure 3). Fold the fabric in half lengthwise two times—this folds the fabric into quarters—to prepare for cutting crosswise strips (figure 4). To cut the fabric into crosswise strips, align the bottom edge of the folded fabric with the mat's grid, lay the ruler over the fabric so the ruler's grid aligns with the mat's grid, and cut the strips with the rotary cutter (figure 5). You'll find rotary cutters easily slice through multiple fabric layers in a single pass.

Pressing

You'll need an iron and ironing board for pressing at every stage of making a quilt. Choose an iron you can use with or without steam, depending on the requirements of the fabric or supplies you are using.

OTHER TOOLS & SUPPLIES

For some quilt projects in this book, you'll need additional items.

Paper-backed fusible web is a sewing product that streamlines the steps for making appliqués (see page 20). This two-ply material feels rough on the fusible web side and smooth on the paper side. The paper is transparent enough to allow you to see a template's outline so you can trace it directly onto the paper. Follow the manufacturer's directions to apply the paper-backed web to the appliqué fabric and peel off the paper backing to fuse the fabric appliqué permanently in place on the quilt.

Freezer paper, a common household product, often is useful when making quilts. One side of the paper has a matte finish, while the other is shiny. Like paper-backed fusible web, freezer paper is transparent

There are many sizes of cutters, rulers, and mats, and you may want to collect several of each over time. To begin making quilts, you will need a cutter in the 45 mm or the smaller 28 mm size, a 24 x 6-inch (61 x 15.2 cm) ruler, and a 24 x 18-inch (61 x 45.7 cm) mat. This size mat will accommodate fabric folded into quarters crosswise for cutting binding strips or any of the appliqués or pieced blocks called for in this book.

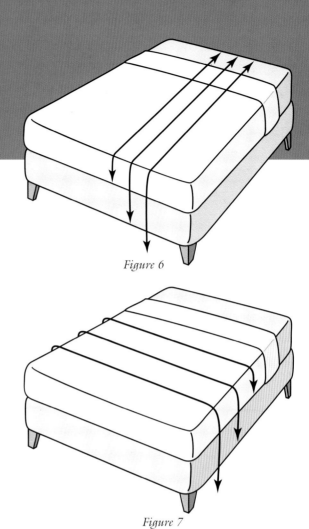

enough to allow you to see the printed outline of a template so you can trace it directly onto the matte side. You can then position the tracing shiny side down on a fabric and use a dry iron to temporarily hold it in place on the fabric.

To mark quilting guidelines or appliqué placement lines on a quilt, use a chalk marker or an evaporating ink marker that is designed especially for use on fabrics. These tools will produce a mark that is temporary and will not stain the quilt.

Quilter's basting spray and fabric glue stick are adhesives that can help you to position appliqués or handle slippery fabrics as you make a quilt. Follow the manufacturer's directions for using these products and to learn the best way to remove them from the completed quilt.

PLANNING A BED QUILT

The finished size of each bed quilt design in this book is given as a guide. Usually you can adapt the size of a quilt design to fit the bed you have in mind by making the quilt top larger or smaller, perhaps by adding or subtracting blocks and borders. Of course, you'll need to increase or decrease the amount of materials accordingly.

To measure a bed, make it up complete with sheets and any blankets. Use a tape measure or steel tape to determine the desired finished length of the quilt—it might drop to the top of the box spring, to the bottom of the box spring, or to the floor (see figure 6). To determine the desired finished width of the quilt, measure across the bed using the same drops—to the top or bottom of the box spring, or to the floor (see figure 7). If you want the finished quilt to cover the bed pillows, put the pillows on the bed and add a tuck-in allowance to the desired finished length as you measure.

Figure 6

Figure 7

Standard Mattress Sizes

A *finished quilt should be wider and longer than the mattress to extend beyond the mattress edges at the foot and sides. Use these standard bed mattress sizes as a rule of thumb when judging the finished size of a quilt: crib, 52 x 27 inches (132.1 x 68.6 cm); twin, 75 x 39 inches (190.5 x 99.1 cm); full/double, 75 x 54 inches (190.5 x 137.2 cm); queen, 80 x 60 inches (203.2 x 152.4 cm); and king, 80 x 76 inches (203.2 x 193 cm).*

A lap throw can be more loosely sized, since it does not fit over a mattress; a common finished throw size is about 60 x 50 inches (152.4 x 127 cm).

PLANNING AN ART QUILT

An art quilt is used as a wall hanging. Compared to a bed quilt or throw, which is designed to be functional, an art quilt is meant to be purely decorative.

The finished size of each art quilt design in this book is given as a guide. Usually you can adapt the size of an art quilt design by making the quilt top larger or smaller, or by adding or subtracting blocks and borders. Of course, you'll need to increase or decrease the amount of materials accordingly.

Sew a Hanging Sleeve

To mount an art quilt on the wall, you will need to sew a hanging sleeve to the backing. A hanging sleeve is a tube of lightweight fabric sewn to the backing in a way that builds some slack into the tube. When you insert a wood dowel in the sleeve to hang the quilt, the slack accommodates the bulk of the dowel and enables the art quilt to hang smoothly.

To sew a sleeve, follow the project instructions to cut a strip of backing fabric or plain muslin shorter than the finished width of the quilt. Fold the short raw ends under ¼ inch (6 mm) two times to make a hem, and

Figure 8

Figure 9

stitch (see figure 8). Fold the sleeve in half along its length with right sides together and stitch a ¼-inch (6 mm) seam, making the sleeve into a tube. Turn the tube right side out, centering the seam on one side (see figure 9).

Sew the top edge of the sleeve, seam side down, by hand to the quilt backing. Pin the bottom edge of the sleeve to the quilt backing so some slack forms in the sleeve (see figure 10). Sew the bottom edge of the sleeve by hand to the quilt backing.

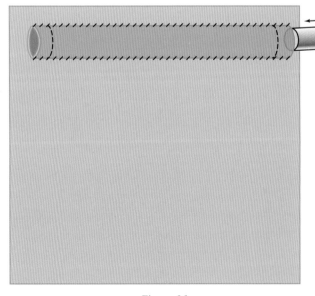

Figure 10

ESSENTIAL MACHINE SEWING TECHNIQUES

Seams

For quilt seams, generally you'll use a ¼-inch (6 mm) seam allowance. Practice with scrap fabric to find the best way to sew this narrow seam accurately on your sewing machine.

On some machine models, the throat plate will be etched with a line you can use to guide the raw edge of the fabric the correct distance from the needle. Perhaps the outside edge of the presser foot can be used to align the fabric. If your machine allows you to change the needle position, move the needle to the left or to the right to find a setting that helps you use the throat plate line or the presser foot edge to sew the seam. If necessary, you can always mark the throat plate temporarily with a strip of masking tape to make your own ¼-inch (6 mm) seam guide.

Usually quilt seams are pressed to one side (see figure 11). This is an easy way to handle the narrow seam allowances, and some experts feel it makes the seam stronger by reducing stress on the stitches. At times the project instructions specify pressing the seam allowances open; this may be necessary to reduce bulk because of the fabrics selected or if the design causes seams to fall on top of one another.

Straight-Stitch Quilting

With a few machine adjustments, the same straight stitch you use to sew the quilt seams can be used to quilt the fabric layers together (see figure 12). This method is the most basic form of machine quilting, and it's easy to accomplish when the quilting path follows straight lines.

Prepare the sewing machine by inserting a sharp, new needle. A regular size 75/11 or 80/12 needle works well when using a low-loft batting and light-weight fabrics for the quilt top and backing. Select a larger size 90/14 needle when working with a loftier batting or heavier fabrics.

To achieve a balanced stitch that looks the same on the quilt top as on the backing, you may need to loosen the needle tension and lengthen the stitch. Use a scrap sandwich of quilt top fabric, batting, and backing fabric to test the machine settings until you are satisfied.

Figure 11

Figure 12

To keep all the quilt layers smooth and free of tiny tucks or puckers as you stitch, use a walking foot attachment (see page 12) or engage the even feed feature (if available on your sewing machine model). Roll and unroll sections of large quilts on the right-hand side of the stitching area to maneuver the rest of the quilt under the arm as you stitch (see figure 13). Secure the roll with safety pins or bicycle clips. Set the machine on a big table to help support the weight of a large quilt as you

stitch, or place some folding tables behind the machine and to its left to extend the work surface. Remove the safety pins used to baste the quilt as you approach them; do not stitch over them.

A quilt bar attachment, added either to a walking foot or a standard presser foot, makes it easy to stitch parallel rows across the entire quilt. Mark and stitch the initial row through the center of the quilt, then let the bar ride on this line as you stitch an even distance on each side of it (see figure 14). For example, to stitch a quilting design of diamonds, simply stitch an "X" to join the diagonal corners, then let the bar ride on each line of the "X" to guide the rows that follow. In a similar way, to stitch a quilted grid of squares, begin by stitching a "+" from the center point of the quilt's opposite edges, then let the bar ride on each line of the "+" to guide the rows that follow.

"Stitch in the ditch" is a catchy nickname for a method of hiding straight-stitch quilting on the top of a quilt. For this technique, use your fingers to spread the quilt along the seamline and guide the needle to place the stitches directly on the seam (see figure 15).

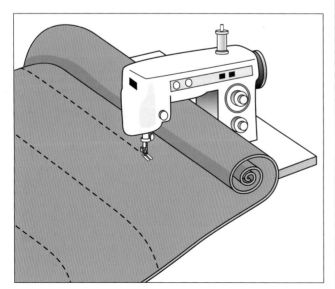

Figure 13

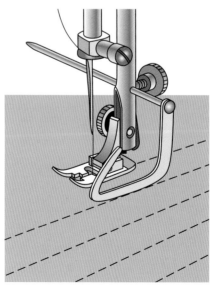

Figure 14

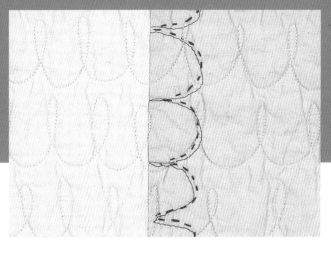

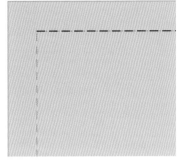

Figure 15   *Figure 16*

Outline quilting, a variation of straight-stitch quilting, means quilting around a design detail on the quilt top (see figure 16). Tracing the outline in this way emphasizes the detail and gives it a subtle dimension. Echo quilting is stitching the outline two or more times in parallel rows.

Free-Motion Quilting

This machine quilting technique takes a little practice to master, but it offers great artistic freedom and does not limit you to stitching in a straight line. That's why many free-motion quilting designs include fluid details such as loops, scrolls, or swirls (see figure 17).

Figure 17

For free-motion stitching, follow the directions in the sewing machine manual to adjust the machine. Generally, you must remove the regular presser foot and attach a darning foot, which has a small, circular opening through which the needle passes (see figure 18). (This foot may also be called a free-motion quilting foot or a darning/embroidery foot.) You'll also need to disengage the feed dogs, which are the teeth under the needle that move the fabric; for your model you may have to either flick a switch to lower the feed dogs, cover the feed dogs with a machine accessory, or set the stitch length to "0".

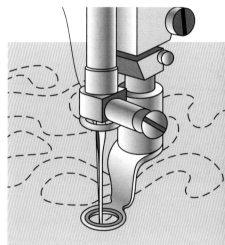

Figure 18

With these two main adjustments, you have set up the machine so the needle sews without the machine moving the fabric. Instead, you control the movement of the fabric by spreading out your fingers and placing a hand on each side of the needle (see figure 19). In this position, you can control the stitch length by moving the quilt layers as quickly or slowly as desired, and you can move them in any direction to create the design you envision.

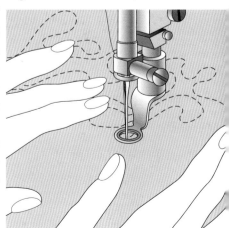

Figure 19

Contemporary Appliqué Methods

Appliqué means cutting out a decorative shape from one fabric and applying it to another fabric. Contemporary appliqué methods are especially easy thanks to fusible products and machine sewing techniques.

Fusible Appliqué

For this method, you will need to purchase paper-backed fusible web that is 17 inches (43.2 cm) wide.

To create an appliqué, use a pencil to trace the pattern onto the paper backing. Note that the finished appliqué will be the reverse of the pattern. Cut out the tracing roughly, leaving a margin around the outline (see figure 20). Follow the manufacturer's directions to fuse the rough-cut tracing, fusible web side down, onto the wrong side of the fabric. Cut out the appliqué on the traced outline (see figure 21). Peel off the paper backing to fuse the appliqué to the right side of the quilt top (see figure 22), once again following the manufacturer's directions.

Follow the project directions to finish the appliqué edges with machine stitching.

Frayed-Edge Appliqué

This easy method exposes the raw edge of the appliqué fabric. As it frays through use, the raw edge blossoms into a soft design detail.

Hold the appliqué temporarily in place on the quilt top with pins, fabric glue stick, or quilter's basting spray. Adjust the sewing machine for straight stitching with a short stitch length, or select a short and narrow zigzag stitch. Stitch a scant ¼ inch (6 mm) from the raw edge (see figure 23).

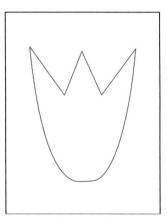

Figure 20

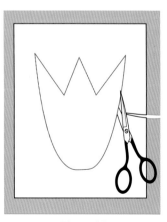

Figure 21

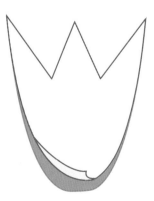

Figure 22

Figure 23

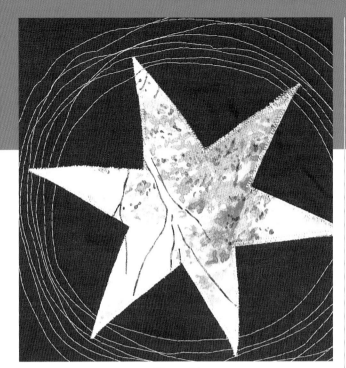

Figure 24

Satin-Stitched Appliqué

Satin stitching means using a dense, uniform zigzag stitch to sew appliqués onto quilts (see figure 24). Follow the directions in the manual for your sewing machine to learn how to adjust the length and width of a zigzag stitch, and test various stitch settings on scrap fabric. Select a length short enough so the stitches form very closely together and look like a solid outline without any fabric showing through the stitches. Select a width that covers the raw edge securely and completely.

ESSENTIAL HAND SEWING TECHNIQUES

Running Stitch

This elementary hand sewing stitch is used for hand quilting and for adding design details. To sew a running stitch, weave the needle in and out of the fabric (see figure 25). For quilting, make the stitches short and even. For design details sewn with a heavy thread such as yarn or floss, make the stitches long and even.

At the beginning of a row of running stitches used for quilting, tie a knot at the end of the thread. To hide the knot, insert the needle through the layers so the knot rests on the quilt top. Pull the thread gently from the backing side until the knot pops through the top and hides in the batting (see figure 26), then trim the thread tail.

To secure the thread at the end of a row of running stitches, tie a knot and insert the needle through the batting, bringing the needle out through the quilt top a short distance away. Pull the thread gently until the knot pops through the top, and trim the thread tail (see figure 27).

Tying

Tying is an easy way to sew the quilt layers together permanently with minimal stitching. Thread a sharp embroidery needle that has a large eye with a long piece of yarn, floss, or perle cotton, and do not knot the end. Take a stitch through all the quilt layers, leaving a long tail, then move to the next tying position to take another stitch without cutting the tail (see figure 28). Cut the tails between the stitches and tie them in a square knot (see figure 29). Trim the tails from ¾ to 1 inch (1.9 to 2.5 cm) in length.

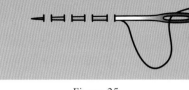

Figure 25

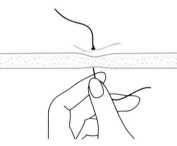

Figure 26

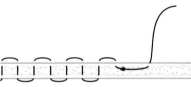

Figure 27

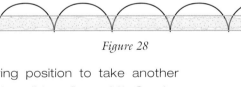

Figure 28

Figure 29

Figure 31

ESSENTIAL QUILT ASSEMBLY TECHNIQUES

Here are the basic steps for assembling your quilt.

Adding a Sashing Strip

Some quilt blocks are joined by sashing strips, which are strips of cloth sewn between each block and each row. Sashing strips form a frame around the quilt blocks. Follow the project instructions to cut and piece the sashing strips.

Figure 30

Attaching a Border

A border, sewn to the edges of the quilt top like an outline or frame, enhances several quilt designs in this book. Follow the project directions to cut fabric strips in the correct size for the border.

After cutting the strips, join the short ends of them with right sides together in a ¼-inch (6 mm) seam, making one long border strip. Press the seams to one side.

Right sides together, stitch the border strip to the top and bottom edges of the quilt top with a ¼-inch (6 mm) seam. Trim the ends of the border strip even with the sides of the quilt top. Press the seam allowances toward the border (see figure 30).

In the same way, stitch a border strip to each side edge of the quilt top (see figure 31).

Stacking and Basting the Quilt Layers

Prepare to stack the quilt layers by pressing the quilt top and backing to remove any wrinkles. Unfold the batting and allow it to relax so it lies flat.

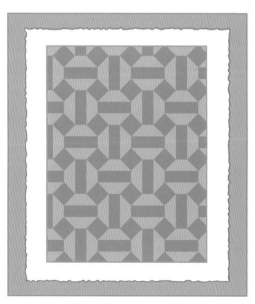

Figure 32

Working on a hard surface large enough to accommodate the quilt, smooth out the backing right side down. Lay the batting on top of the backing, then place the quilt top, right side up, on top of the batting (see figure 32). The project instructions, in most cases, will direct you to cut the batting larger than the quilt top and the backing larger than the batting; stack the layers so an equal margin of batting and backing shows all around.

Working from the center of the quilt out toward the edges, baste the layers together with safety pins. Space the pins about 6 inches (15.2 cm) apart. Check the basted quilt from the back to be sure it's smooth, with no pleats or puckers.

Binding a Quilt

A binding is a strip of fabric used to encase the raw edges of the quilt layers. It's the final step in making almost every quilt design in this book.

Preparation

Prepare the quilt for binding by trimming it evenly so the edges of the quilt top, batting, and backing align. Use a rotary cutter, ruler, and mat to trim the corners at a right angle.

Follow the project instructions to cut strips of fabric for binding the quilt. Join them into one long binding strip by overlapping the short ends at right angles, with right sides together, then sewing a diagonal seam across the corner; trim the seam allowance to ¼ inch (6 mm)(see figure 33). Press the seams open to minimize bulk.

Stitching

With right sides together and working from the quilt top, stitch the binding to the quilt layers with either mitered or butted corners, as stated in the project directions.

Figure 33

MITERED CORNERS

Start applying the binding to the quilt near one corner. Fold the short raw edge on the diagonal ¼ inch (6 mm) to the wrong side to start (see figure 34). Using the seam allowance given in the project instructions, begin stitching the binding.

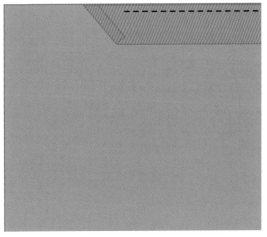

Figure 34

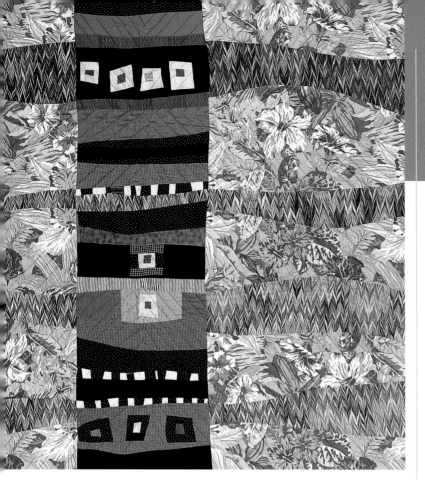

When you come to the starting point as you near the end of the binding, lap the end of the binding strip over the folded raw edge (see figure 37) to complete stitching the binding seam.

Once the binding is stitched around the entire edge of the quilt, fold the binding over the raw edges of all the quilt layers to bring the binding to the quilt backing. Turn under the long raw edge of the binding so the fold just covers the stitches from the binding seam. Work the binding corners with your fingertips to fold a miter—a fold that forms a 45-degree angle—on the quilt top and on the backing; pin the miters. Slipstitch the folded-under raw edge of the binding to the backing by hand (see figure 38), or stitch in the ditch of the binding seam from the quilt top by machine (see page 18).

At each corner, stop stitching away from the corner a distance equal to the seam allowance. Take one or two backstitches to lock the seam, clip the threads, and remove the quilt from the sewing machine. Fold the binding straight up so a 45-degree angle forms in the binding (see figure 35). Fold the binding straight down so it is even with the edge of the quilt, and resume stitching (see figure 36).

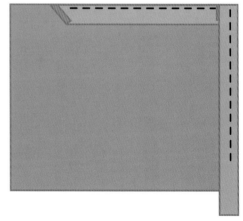

Figure 36

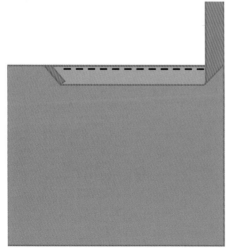

Figure 35

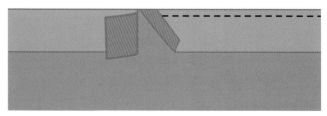

Figure 37

BUTTED CORNERS

Stitch the binding to the top and bottom edges of the quilt, using the seam allowance given in the project directions. Trim the binding even with the side edges of the quilt. Fold the binding over the raw edge of the quilt backing. Turn under the raw edge of the binding so the folded edge just covers the stitches from the binding seam. Slipstitch the fold to the backing by hand, as shown in figure 38, or stitch in the ditch of the binding seam by machine, working from the quilt top side.

In the same way, stitch the binding to each of the side edges of the quilt, but trim the binding so it is ¼ inch (6 mm) longer than the edges of the quilt to allow you to fold under the binding raw edges at the ends (see figure 39). As when binding the shorter edges, turn under the long raw edge of the binding and slipstitch the fold or stitch in the ditch. Slipstitch the ends of the binding closed.

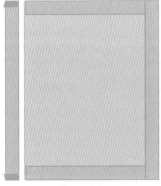

Figure 38

Figure 39

Sewing a Double-Layer Binding

When you expect a quilt to receive regular use and frequent launderings, the double-layer binding option will give you a durable finish. Cut the binding strips six times the finished width— for example, cut the binding strips 1½ inches (3.8 cm) wide for a binding that measures ¼ inch (6mm) once finished, or cut the binding strips 3 inches (7.6 cm) wide for a binding that measures ½ inch (1.3 cm) once finished.

Figure 40

After joining the strips into one long binding strip with diagonal seams, fold the strip in half along its length with wrong sides together and press (see figure 40). Apply the folded binding with mitered or butted corners on the right side of the quilt, placing the raw edges together. Use a seam allowance just a scant amount less than the finished width to allow for turn of cloth. Slipstitch the pressed fold to the quilt backing or stitch in the ditch of the binding seam from the quilt top.

Now that you've become acquainted with the basics of creating contemporary quilts, you're ready to choose your favorite quilt designs from the following pages and start sewing. You'll find the process creative, exciting, and rewarding, even if this is the first time you've ever made a quilt.

THE
QUILTS

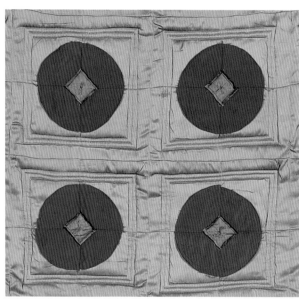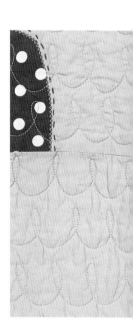

T he contemporary aesthetic found in the 20 quilt designs that follow results from modern techniques, innovative fabrics, and imaginative stitching.

SPARROW

RACHEL FIELDS

DESIGNER

Give this easy wall hanging a folk art flavor by leaving the edges of the appliqués unfinished and stitching the sparrow outline roughly with contrasting thread. For a quick finish, instead of sewing a separate binding, simply line the quilt top to the edge.

Finished size: approximately 20 inches (50.8 cm) square

22 x 20-inch (55.9 x 50.8 cm)
piece of red velvet fabric

20 x 6-inch (50.8 cm x 15.2 cm) strip
of red print fabric

22 x 2-inch (55.9 x 5.1 cm) strip of
gold brocade fabric

BACKING:

24-inch (61 cm) square of
gray printed fabric

APPLIQUÉ:

2½ x 2 inch (6.4 x 5.1 cm) oval of
turquoise fabric

THREAD, ETC:

Ecru sewing thread

1³⁄₁₆ inch (3 cm) white/gold
shank button

11 x 2½-inch (27.9 x 6.4 cm) strip of
cotton fabric for the hanging sleeve

12-inch (30.5 cm) wood dowel,
¼ inch (6 mm) in diameter

SUPPLIES

Freezer paper

TEMPLATE

See page 120

½-inch (1.3 cm) seam allowance

DESIGNER'S NOTE: This quilt
presents an opportunity to use
decorative sewing machine
stitches, especially stitch patterns
that are light and airy. If desired,
you could select a zigzag
stitch as a substitute.

INSTRUCTIONS

1 Place the strip of red print fabric 3 inches (7.6 cm) from the left side of the red velvet fabric; do not turn under the edges of the fabric strip. Adjust the sewing machine for a decorative stitch, threading the needle and filling the bobbin with ecru thread. Stitch next to the raw edges of the red print fabric.

2 Place the strip of brocade fabric along the bottom edge of the red velvet fabric, with the velvet fabric overlapping by about ¼ inch (6 mm). Use a decorative or wide zigzag stitch to sew the pieces together.

3 Trace the template onto the matte side of freezer paper to make the sparrow stitching pattern.

4 Place the pattern shiny side down on the wrong side of the velvet section of the quilt top. Press the pattern lightly with a dry iron to baste the pattern in position. Adjust the sewing machine for straight stitching. Stitch on the pattern to transfer the sparrow outline to the right side of the quilt top. Remove the pattern.

5 Stack the print backing fabric and the quilt top with right sides together. Trim the backing fabric even with the edges of the quilt top. Stitch around the edges using a ½-inch (1.3 cm) seam allowance and leaving a 2-inch (5.1 cm) opening along the bottom edge.

6 Trim the seam allowances diagonally across the corners to reduce bulk. Turn the quilt right side out through the opening. Press under the seam allowances at the edges. Sew the opening closed by hand.

7 Adjust the sewing machine for a decorative stitch and stitch around the edge of the quilt.

8 Adjust the sewing machine for a straight stitch. Working from the right side of the quilt, stitch the sparrow outline several times, following the outline roughly to add character to the stitching.

9 Place the oval of turquoise fabric near the upper right corner of the quilt top. Stitch around the fabric oval several times.

10 Sew the button near the center of the oval.

11 Attach the hanging sleeve.

12 Insert the dowel into the sleeve to hang the quilt.

FLICKA

HILLARY LANG

DESIGNER

Thanks to the mix of prints used for the appliqués and the way they're arranged, this quilt has a carefree feeling. To finish the quilt, you can line it with the backing and skip the step of applying a separate binding.

Finished size: approximately 58 x 41 inches (147.3 x 104.1 cm)

MATERIALS

QUILT TOP:

1¾ yards (1.6 m) of solid cotton fabric for the quilt top, 45 inches (114.3 cm) wide

APPLIQUÉS:

¼ yard (.2 m) each of about 25 assorted cotton print fabrics

BACKING:

1¾ yards (1.6 m) of cotton print fabric, 45 inches (114.3 cm) wide

BATTING:

Low-loft cotton batting, 59 x 42 inches (149.9 x 106.7 cm)

THREAD:

Sewing thread to match the quilt top fabric

TOOLS

Quilter's safety pins

¼-inch (6 mm) seam allowance

DESIGNER'S NOTE: Indulge your love of fabric and personalize this quilt by collecting small fabric pieces with storybook motifs, geometric designs, cartoons, barnyard animals, and any other prints you find appealing. Placing the appliqués for a balanced look is the key to this quilt design. To judge the balance, step a room's length away and squint at the arrangement. If the same prints appear too close together or you notice any concentrations of color, rearrange the patches.

INSTRUCTIONS

1 Cut about two or three squares or rectangles from each of the assorted cotton print fabrics for the appliqués. Cut them so the edges measure between 6 and 8 inches (15.2 and 20.3 cm) in size. Cut them freehand so the appliqués look charmingly imperfect.

2 Turn under the raw edges of each appliqué ¼ inch (6 mm), and press.

3 Trim the quilt top fabric to 59 x 42 inches (149.9 x 106.7 cm). Spread it out flat with the right side up.

4 Begin placing the appliqués in a border about 4 to 6 (10.2 to 15.2 cm) inches from the edge of the quilt top; space the border appliqués about 6 to 8 inches (15.2 to 20.3 cm) apart, tilting them at different angles. Place the next row of appliqués in the same way, overlapping the border; leave open areas so the quilt top fabric shows through. Continue in the same way to cover the quilt top with a balanced arrangement of appliqués. Adjust the overlapping edges of the appliqués so no appliqué is completely under or on top of its neighbors. Baste the appliqués to the quilt top with safety pins, pinning each appliqué through the center and at every overlapping corner.

5 Adjust the sewing machine to make a zigzag stitch of medium length and narrow width. Thread the needle and fill the bobbin with thread to match the quilt top fabric. Stitch along the edges of each appliqué, keeping the quilt top flat and smooth and removing the safety pins as you go.

6 Trim the backing fabric to 59 x 42 inches (149.9 x 106.7 cm).

7 Stack the quilt layers, beginning with the quilt top right side up. Lay the backing wrong side up on the quilt top. Place the batting on top of the backing. Pin the layers together near the edge all around. Trim the edges so the layers are even.

8 Adjust the sewing machine for straight stitching. Stitch the quilt layers together around the outer edges using a ½-inch (1.3 cm) seam allowance and leaving an 8-inch (20.3 cm) opening along one edge.

9 Trim the quilt layers across the corners to reduce bulk (see figure 1). Trim the batting seam allowance close to the stitching. Turn the quilt right side out through the opening. Turn under the raw edges along the opening and sew the opening closed by hand.

10 Smooth out the quilt so the layers are even. Baste the layers together with safety pins.

11 Adjust the sewing machine for straight-stitch quilting. Begin at the center of one long edge to stitch straight across the quilt. Attach a quilting bar to the sewing machine to stitch the remaining rows parallel to the first and spaced 2½ inches (6.4 cm) apart.

Figure 1

THE SQUARE ROOT OF
YIN+
YANG

XAVORA FISHER

DESIGNER

This intriguing quilt takes its name from the positive-negative effect you can achieve by playing with a pair of colors. The color play begins with the diagonally pieced top, continues with the appliqués, and extends all the way to the edges of the quilt with a wide, pieced binding.

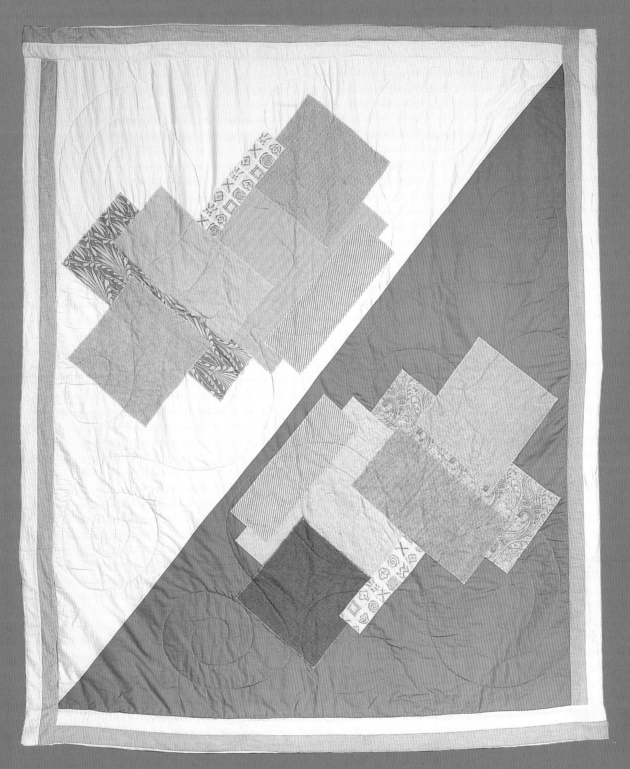

Finished size: approximately 86 x 72 inches (218.4 x 182.9 cm)

MATERIALS

QUILT TOP AND BACKING:

2¼ yards (2.1 m) of neutral cotton sheeting fabric, 110 inches (279.4 cm) wide (color A)

2¼ yards (2.1 m) of contrasting cotton sheeting fabric, 110 inches (279.4 cm) wide

APPLIQUÉS:

Fourteen 25 x 15-inch (63.5 x 38.1 cm) pieces of assorted fabrics, seven to coordinate with one sheeting fabric color and seven to coordinate with the other sheeting fabric color

BINDING:

Additional ¼ yard (0.2 m) each of two of the contrasting appliqué fabrics (colors B and C)

BATTING:

Low-loft batting, 90 x 76 inches (228.6 x 193 cm)

THREAD:

Neutral sewing thread

TOOLS & SUPPLIES

Quilt basting spray

Disappearing ink fabric marker

¼-inch (6 mm) seam allowance

DESIGNER'S NOTE: Select appliqué fabrics with different textures such as piqué, corduroy, and flannel, and mix them with some tone-on-tone broadcloth prints to add interest to the quilt.

INSTRUCTIONS

1 Prewash all fabrics.

2 Trim each sheeting fabric for the quilt top and backing to 78½ x 64½ inches (199.4 x 163.8 cm), reserving the excess for the binding. Stack the two fabric layers with the right sides facing up and the edges aligned. Cut through both layers from one corner diagonally to the opposite corner.

3 Stitch each pair of contrasting sections with right sides together in a diagonal seam to make two positive-negative panels (see figure 1). Press the seams to one side. Use one panel for the quilt top and reserve the other for the backing.

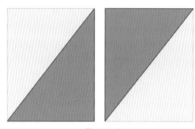
Figure 1

4 Cut matching sizes and shapes of appliqués from each set of assorted fabrics, making the largest appliqué in each set about 25 x 15 inches (63.5 x 38.1 cm). Feel free to experiment with the shapes and sizes of the appliqués to create a pleasing arrangement of overlapping layers.

5 Use a disappearing ink fabric marker to mark the center of the diagonal seam on the quilt top. Draw a line from this mark to the opposite corners as a guide for arranging each set of appliqués in a mirror-image design next to the diagonal seam (see figure 2). Following the manufacturer's directions, apply basting spray to the wrong side of each appliqué to hold it in place on the quilt top.

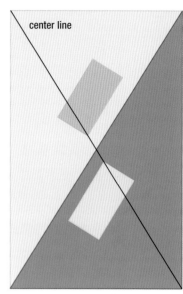
center line

Figure 2

6 Adjust the sewing machine for satin-stitch appliqué. Stitch around the edges of each appliqué.

7 Stack and baste the quilt layers. Make sure the batting extends beyond the top and backing by an even margin all around.

8 Adjust the sewing machine for straight-stitch quilting. Stitch a design of large, circular swirls on one half of the quilt top. On the other half of the quilt top, stitch a mirror-image design of large, circular swirls.

9 Trim the quilt layers so the batting extends beyond the edges of the top and backing by a margin of 4 inches (10.2 cm) all around.

10 Cut four 4½ x 91-inch (11.4 x 231.1 cm) binding strips from the reserved neutral sheeting fabric—this fabric will be called color A. Cut the following 2½ x 91-inch (6.4 x 231.1 cm) binding strips from the three sheeting colors: four from color A, two from color B, and two from color C. Stitch two of the narrow binding strips to each wide binding strip in the color sequence shown (see figure 3). Press the seams to one side.

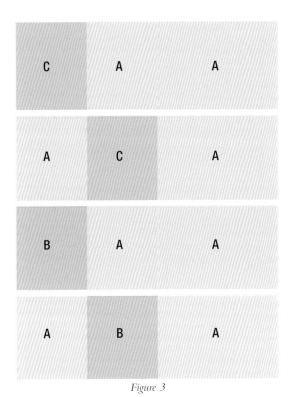

Figure 3

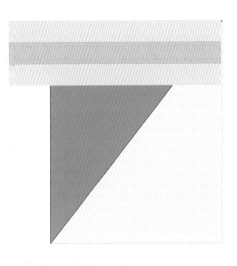

Figure 4

11 Attach the binding strips to the sides of the quilt that feature the contrasting color of appliqués. Fold under the short raw edge of the first binding strip ¼ inch (6 mm) and place it right side down on the quilt backing as shown in figure 4. Trim the strip to fit from the edge of the batting to the edge of the quilt top. Begin stitching 4 inches (10.2 cm) in from the end of the strip, using a ¼-inch (6 mm) seam allowance. Fold the binding strip over the batting to the quilt top. Fold under the long raw edge of the binding strip ¼ inch (6 mm). Adjust the sewing machine for a medium decorative or zigzag stitch. Stitch the lower edge of the binding (see figure 5), stopping at the edge of the quilt top. In the same way, sew a binding strip to each remaining edge of the quilt, but stitch the entire seam without leaving 4 inches (10.2 cm) free at the beginning (see figure 6). Fold the 4 inches (10.2 cm) left free at the beginning of the first binding strip over the end of the final binding strip. Close the open ends of the binding strips with hand stitches.

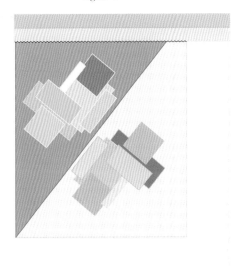

Figure 5

12 Launder the quilt to remove the basting spray.

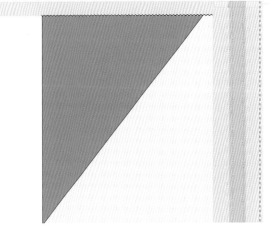

Figure 6

SPACE AGE LOUNGE

JEN SWEARINGTON

DESIGNER

This luxurious silk shantung quilt does not require precision—in fact, it encourages improvisation. The idea is to play with layers of sheer fabrics and create an arrangement you find exciting.

Finished size: approximately 84 x 76½ inches (213.4 x 194.3 cm)

MATERIALS

QUILT TOP AND BACKING:

7½ yards (6.9 m) of blue silk shantung fabric, 54 inches (137.2 cm) wide

APPLIQUÉS:

2 yards (1.8 m) of black silk organza, 44 inches (111.8 cm) wide

½ (0.5 m) yard of white silk organza, 44 inches (111.8 cm) wide

1 yard (0.9 m) of gold silk or polyester organza, 60 inches (152.4 cm) wide

1 yard (0.9 m) of metallic copper sheer fabric, 44 inches (111.8 cm) wide

BINDING:

1 yard (0.9 m) of black fabric, 45 inches (114.3 cm) wide

BATTING:

Fusible cotton blend quilt batting, 88 x 80½ inches (223.5 x 204.5 cm)

THREAD, ETC:

Black heavy-duty cotton/polyester thread

Bulky red acrylic yarn

Blue sewing thread

Clear monofilament nylon thread

Bulky red acrylic yarn

TOOLS

Quilter's safety pins

Embroidery needle with a large eye

Chalk fabric marker

¼-inch (6 mm) seam allowance

INSTRUCTIONS

1 Cut off the selvages from the blue shantung fabric. Cut the fabric crosswise into six pieces, each 45 inches (114.3 cm) long. Cut two of these pieces in half lengthwise so they measure 45 x 27 inches (114.3 x 68.6 cm).

2 Sew one 45-inch (114.3 cm) edge of each full-width piece to one 45 inch (114.3 cm) edge of a half-width piece with right sides together. Press each seam open.

3 Sew each pair of seamed pieces with right sides together, rotating one of the pieces so the seams are staggered (see figure 1). Press the seams open. Trim one of these seamed pieces to 84 x 76½ inches (213.4 x 194.3 cm) and use it for the quilt top. Trim the other seamed piece to 89 x 81½ inches (226.1 x 207 cm) and reserve it for the backing.

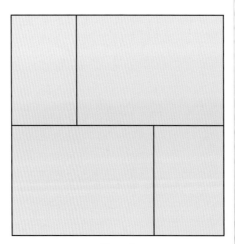

Figure 1

DESIGNER'S NOTE: Silk fabrics come in various widths, so you'll need to purchase extra fabric if your selections are not as wide as those listed at the left. The bridal and eveningwear departments of fabric shops are good places to find the materials you'll need.

4 Cut out various sizes and shapes of large appliqués from the black, white, gold, and copper fabrics. As a guide, for the quilt shown the following rectangle appliqués were cut from black organza fabric: one 40 x 32 inches (101.6 x 81.3 cm), one 7 x 10½ inches (17.8 x 26.7 cm), and one 7 x 5½ inches (17.8 x 14 cm); also a rough oval 13½ x 18 1/2 inches (34.3 x 47 cm). The following rectangle appliqués were cut from gold organza fabric: one 14 x 56 inches (35.6 x 142.2 cm) and one 23½ x 21 inches (59.7 x 53.3 cm). The following rectangle appliqués were cut from copper fabric: one 20 x 28 inches (50.8 x 71.1 cm), one 15 x 12 inches (38.1 x 30.5 cm), and one 3 x 13 inches (7.6 x 33 cm). The quilt has two leaf shapes 8 x 15 inches (20.3 x 38.1 cm) cut from white organza fabric.

5 Lay the quilt top right side up on a smooth, flat surface. Arrange the appliqués so they overlap as desired. Pin the edges of the appliqués to the quilt top about every 2 inches (5.1 cm) all around.

6 Adjust the sewing machine to sew a straight stitch. Thread the needle with heavy-duty black thread and fill the bobbin with blue thread. Begin stitching at the center of one long edge of the quilt top and stitch across to the opposite edge, removing the pins as you go. Stitch ¼ to ½ inch (6 mm to 1.3 cm) inside the edge of each appliqué you encounter, securing the raw appliqué edges and creating a black line of stitches leading from one appliqué to another. In the same way, begin at the center of one short edge of the quilt top background and stitch toward the opposite edge. Continue stitching from edge to edge over the quilt top until all the appliqué edges have been stitched securely.

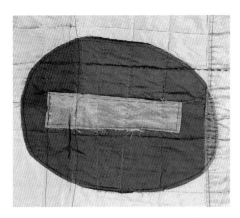

7 Thread the embroidery needle with a long piece of red yarn. Sew several rows of running stitches spaced across the width and along the length of the quilt top. For each row, begin at one edge of the quilt top and leave a 2-inch (5.1 cm) tail of yarn. At the opposite edge of the quilt top, cut the yarn to leave a 2-inch (5.1 cm) tail.

8 Use the chalk fabric marker to draw a line from the center of each edge of the quilt top to the center of the opposite edge as a guideline for the first two rows of quilt stitching.

9 Stack the quilt layers. Follow the manufacturer's directions to fuse the batting to the quilt backing and quilt top. Baste the layers together with safety pins.

10 Adjust the sewing machine for straight-stitch quilting. Thread the needle with clear monofilament nylon thread. Following one of the chalk-marked guidelines, begin at the edge of the quilt to stitch straight across to the opposite edge. If you encounter an appliqué edge as you stitch, adjust the sewing machine for a zigzag stitch to secure the raw edge, then adjust the sewing machine for a straight stitch to continue sewing on the marked guidelines. In the same way, zigzag stitch over the red yarn stitches as you encounter them. Return to straight stitching when you encounter the blue silk background fabric. In this way, cover the entire quilt with vertical and horizontal rows of stitches spaced about 4 to 6 inches (10.2 to 15.2 cm) apart to form a grid.

11 Adjust the sewing machine for zigzag stitching. Thread the needle with black or blue thread. Examine the quilt top and stitch over any raw appliqué edges missed when you stitched the grid. Also zigzag stitch over the red yarn stitches you missed.

12 Cut 1½-inch (3.8 cm) strips crosswise from the black fabric. Bind the quilt, making a double-layer binding with mitered corners and using a ¼-inch (6 mm) seam allowance.

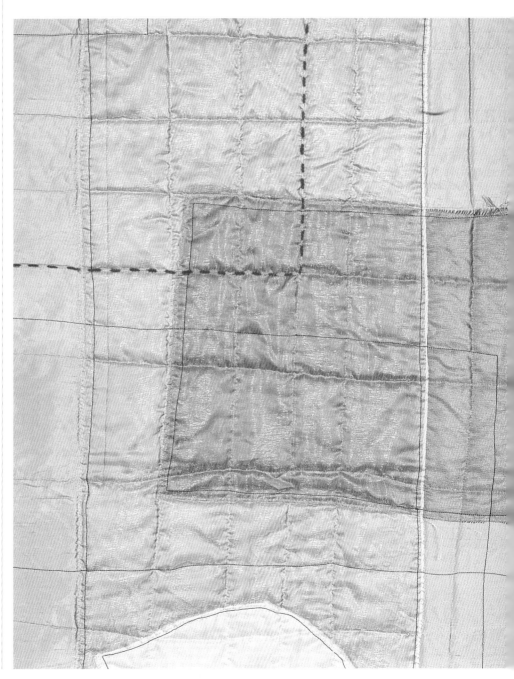

TUMBLING LEAVES

JUDE STUECKER
DESIGNER

Explore the third dimension in quilt making with these fanciful leaf appliqués. They're made from layers of unusual fabrics such as synthetic suede, mesh, and textured upholstery cloth. Each leaf is topstitched to the quilt through its center only, so the edges remain free.

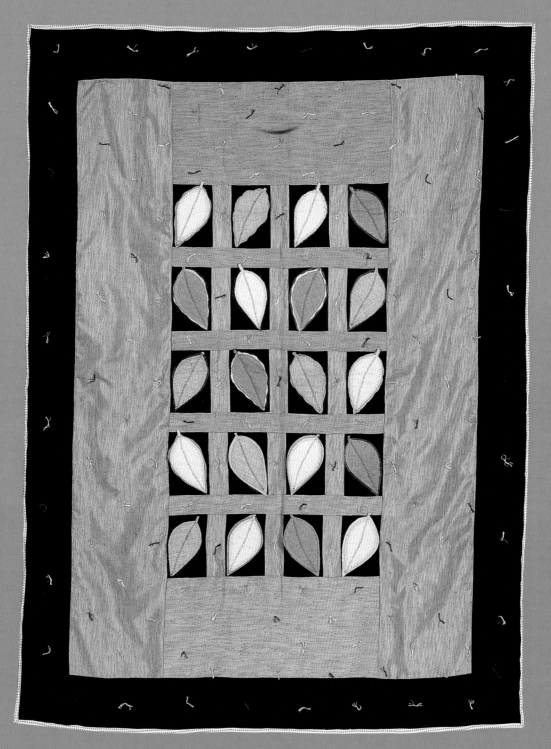

Finished size: approximately 67 x 50 inches (170.2 x 127 cm)

QUILT BLOCKS AND OUTER BORDER:

1½ yards (1.4 m) of dark green wool fabric, 45 inches (114.3 cm) wide

SASHING AND INNER BORDER:

1½ yards (1.4 m) of light green fabric, 45 inches (114.3 cm) wide

APPLIQUÉS:

⅜ yard (0.3 m) each of three assorted textured fabrics, 54 inches (137.2 cm) wide

¼ yard (0.2 m) each of four or five nonwoven fabrics for the leaf contrast, in various widths from 45 to 72 inches wide (114.3 to 182.9 cm)

2 yards (1.8 m) of nonwoven fusible interfacing, 22 inches (55.9 cm) wide

BACKING AND BINDING:

2½ yards (2.3 m) of plaid cotton fabric, 54 inches (137.2 cm) wide

BATTING:

Low-loft batting, 71 x 54 inches (180.3 x 137.2 cm)

THREAD, ETC:

Assorted colors of sewing threads

Four skeins of assorted colors of embroidery floss

TOOLS & SUPPLIES

Embroidery needle with a large eye

Freezer paper

TEMPLATES

See page 121

¼-inch (6 mm) seam allowance

INSTRUCTIONS

1 Cut 20 quilt blocks each measuring 4½ x 6½ inches (11.4 x 16.5 cm) from the dark green wool fabric. Reserve the remaining fabric for the outer border.

2 Cut 15 sashing strips that are each 2½ x 6½ inches (6.4 x 16.5 cm) and four sashing strips that are each 2½ x 16½ inches (6.4 x 41.9 cm) from the light green fabric. Reserve the remaining fabric for the inner border.

3 Sew the blocks into five rows. Each row should have four blocks with a 2½ x 6½-inch (6.4 x 16.5 cm) sashing strip in between the blocks (see figure 1). Press the seams toward the blocks.

4 Sew the rows together with a 2½ x 16½-inch (6.4 x 41.9 cm) sashing strip in between (see figure 2) to make the quilt top. Press the seams toward the blocks.

5 Cut 5½-inch (14 cm) outer border strips crosswise from the reserved wool fabric and 10½-inch (26.7 cm) inner border strips crosswise from the reserved light green fabric. Attach the inner border, then the outer border to the quilt top.

6 Trace Template A 20 times onto the matte side of the fusible interfacing. Turn the template over and trace it 20 more times onto the matte side of fusible interfacing. Cut out the tracings roughly, leaving a margin of interfacing

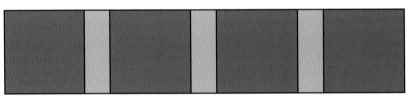

Figure 1

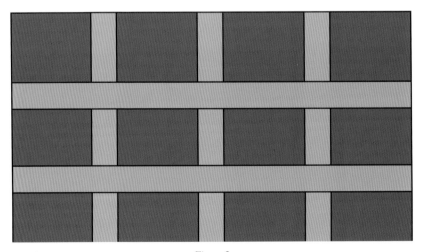

Figure 2

all around. Follow the manufacturer's directions to fuse each traced leaf and traced mirror-image leaf to the wrong side of the textured fabrics to make 20 pairs of matching leaves. Cut out each leaf and mirror-image leaf on the traced outline.

7 Trace Template B onto freezer paper. Cut out the template on the traced outline. Cut the template 20 times from nonwoven fabrics.

8 Stack each pair of matching leaves with the interfaced sides together. Place a leaf contrast section in between (figure 3), with an even margin of the contrast section showing all around the edges. Thread the sewing machine needle and fill the bobbin with one of the assorted colors of sewing threads. Set up the sewing machine for zigzag stitching. Stitch around the edge of each leaf, changing the thread color for each leaf as desired.

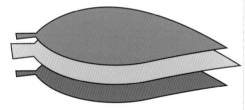

Figure 3

DESIGNER'S NOTE: For the leaves, select upholstery fabrics with interesting weaves and textures. For the leaf contrast, select a mix of novel nonwoven fabrics such as synthetic suede, felt, tulle, and mesh. For yet another surprising use of fabric, choose wool for the quilt blocks and border.

9 Arrange each leaf on a block, placing the leaves at various angles for a tumbling effect. Topstitch each leaf along its center, using a decorative machine stitch or a zigzag stitch and changing the thread color with each leaf as desired.

10 Cut four 1-inch (2.5 cm) crosswise strips from plaid fabric and reserve for the binding. Trim the remaining plaid fabric to 72 x 54 inches (182.9 x 137.2 cm) for the quilt backing.

11 Stack and baste the quilt layers.

12 Tie the quilt about every 6 inches (15.2 cm) with floss.

13 Bind the quilt, using a ¼-inch (6 mm) seam allowance and mitered corners.

EASY CHENILLE

JOAN K.
MORRIS

DESIGNER

As you make this crib quilt, you'll give ordinary cotton muslin a fascinating makeover. After stitching many layers of muslin and batting together, cutting through selected layers, and treating them to a tumble in the clothes dryer, a soft, fluffy texture appears.

Finished size: approximately 48½ x 37½ inches (123.2 x 95.3 cm)

MATERIALS

BLOCKS:

10 yards (9.1 m) of white cotton muslin fabric 37 to 45 inches (94 to 114.3 cm) wide or 6¾ yards (6.2 m), 50 to 58 inches (127 to 147.3 cm) wide

GEOMETRIC SHAPES:

¼ yard (0.2 m) each of blue, yellow, and pink cotton fabrics with color on both faces, 45 inches (114.3 cm) wide

BINDING AND BACKING STRIPS:

1½ (1.4 m) yards of cotton plaid fabric, 45 inches (114.3 cm) wide

BATTING:

Low-loft batting, 60 x 45 inches (152.4 x 114.3 cm)

THREAD:

Six spools of white cotton machine-quilting thread

Sewing thread to blend with the plaid fabric

TOOLS & SUPPLIES

Tracing paper

Fabric glue stick

Chenille rotary cutter or sharp sewing scissors

Warm water

Clothes dryer

TEMPLATES

See page 122

¼-inch (6 mm) seam allowance unless otherwise noted

INSTRUCTIONS

1 Cut forty-eight 15-inch (38.1 cm) squares of muslin and twelve 15-inch (38.1 cm) squares of batting.

2 Stack the following layers for each of the 12 blocks: one muslin square, right side down; one batting square; and three muslin squares, right sides up. Pin through all the layers at each corner.

3 Cut out Templates A, B, and C four times each from blue, yellow, and pink fabric.

4 On a work surface, arrange the pinned blocks in four rows, with three blocks in each row. Place a square, circle, and triangle on each block, varying the arrangement of the colors and shapes on the blocks. Use fabric glue stick to baste each square, circle, and triangle in place.

5 Adjust the sewing machine for a medium straight stitch. Thread the needle and fill the bobbin with white quilting thread. Attach a walking foot or engage the even-feed feature on the sewing machine. On each block, stitch from one corner diagonally to the opposite corner, backstitching at the start and finish to lock the stitches. Pivot the block to stitch diagonally ¼ inch (6 mm)

DESIGNER'S NOTE: A chenille rotary cutter is a timesaving tool for this project—it has a narrow plastic tongue, which slips between the rows of stitches and protects the bottom fabric layers of each block as you cut through the top layers. Most fabric stores and quilt specialty shops carry this tool; you may also find it for sale in some craft stores.

from the first row in the opposite direction, backstitching to lock the stitches (see figure 1). Continue to stitch parallel rows ¼ inch (6 mm) apart on one half of the block, then stitch rows on the other half of the block in the same way.

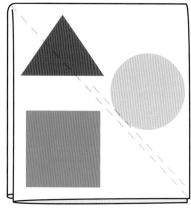

Figure 1

6 Cut the top two muslin layers of each block between the stitched rows, including the circle, triangle, and square shapes as you cut. Do not cut through the batting and the bottom two muslin layers.

7 Dampen each block with warm water. Rub the blocks to open up the cuts between the stitched rows. Put the blocks in a clothes dryer set on high heat. Once dry, the cut edges of each block will fray softly.

8 Trim each block to 12½ inches (31.8 cm) square.

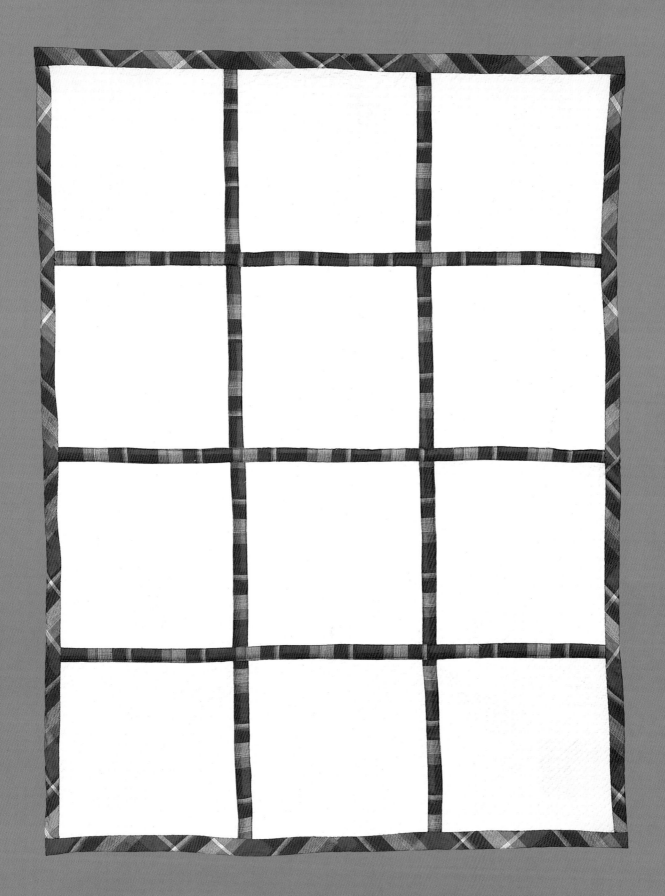

9 Stitch the blocks with right sides together to form rows as described in step 4. Press the seams open. Stitch the rows together, and press the seams open.

10 Cut five 2-inch (5.1 cm) strips crosswise from plaid fabric, reserving the remaining fabric for the binding. Trim three of the strips to 37 inches (94 cm) long, reserving the trimmings. Sew one trimming to each of the two remaining strips with right sides together. Press the seams open. Trim each pieced strip to 49 inches (124.5 cm) long. Fold under each long raw edge on each strip ½ inch (1.3 cm), and press.

11 Thread the sewing machine needle with thread that blends with the plaid fabric, but put white thread in the bobbin. Place the strips over the raw seam allowances on the quilt backing, beginning with the longer strips. Stitch close to the edges of each strip through all layers. Place the shorter strips over the remaining seam allowances (see figure 2). Stitch close to the edges of each strip.

12 Cut the remaining plaid fabric into 2-inch (5.1 cm) strips on the true bias grain (see figure 3). Bind the quilt, using ½-inch (1.3 cm) seam allowances and mitered corners.

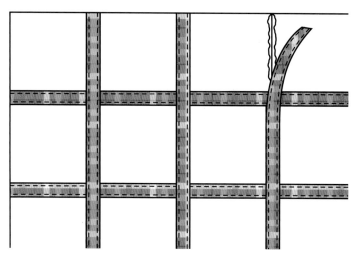

Figure 2

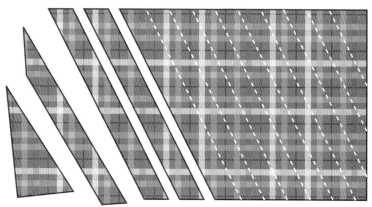

Figure 3

RETRO SASHIKO

KAREN
JAMES SWING

DESIGNER

In traditional sashiko, running stitches made with heavy white thread join fabric layers together. Here the technique gets a new twist by using a rainbow of threads to echo the colors and motifs in the large-scale fabric print used to make the quilt top.

Finished size: approximately 90 x 72 inches (228.6 x 182.9 cm)

INSTRUCTIONS

1 Cut 108 blocks, each 8 inches (20.3 cm) square, from the large-scale circle print fabric.

2 Arrange the blocks into 12 rows with nine blocks in each row. Shift and rotate the blocks to create a pleasing arrangement that balances whole and partial print circles with blocks showing mainly the background color of the print. Use 1/2-inch (1.3 cm) seam allowances to sew the blocks together in rows. Press the seam allowances open. Keeping the pleasing arrangement of blocks in mind, sew the rows together to make the quilt top.

3 For the border, cut crosswise strips 5 inches (12.7 cm) wide from striped fabric. Attach the border.

4 Trim the backing fabric to 99 x 77 inches (251.5 x 195.6 cm).

5 Stack and baste the quilt layers.

DESIGNER'S NOTE: For this quilt, you'll need two home decorating fabrics—a large circle print and a coordinating printed stripe. The size of the quilt's square blocks matches the size of the largest circle motifs, which is about 7 inches (17.8 cm) in diameter. Thus, the blocks are cut 8 inches (20.3 cm) square to allow 1/2-inch (1.3 cm) seam allowances. To adapt this quilt design for print motifs of other sizes, cut the square block 1 inch (2.5 cm) larger than the motif and increase or reduce the number of blocks accordingly to piece the quilt top.

6 Thread the embroidery needle with two strands of one of the assorted colors of floss. Sew large running stitches, about four to five per inch (2.5 cm), through all layers. Sew in paths that echo the shapes of the printed circles, sometimes meandering from one block to another and at other times stopping at the edge of the quilt blocks. The stitch lines can run parallel to one another in some areas and crisscross in others (see figure 1). Change the color of floss frequently to add variety and detail to the stitching. At the border, sew running stitches along the edges of the stripes (see figure 2). Space the lines of running stitches uniformly far apart throughout the quilt.

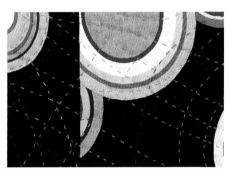

Figure 1

Figure 2

7 Cut 2-inch (5.1 cm) strips crosswise from the small circle print fabric. Bind the quilt, using a 1/2-inch (1.3 cm) seam allowance and mitered corners.

MATERIALS

BLOCKS:

3½ yards (3.2 m) of a large-scale circle print cotton decorator fabric, 54 inches (137.2 cm) wide

BORDER:

½ (0.5 m) yard of striped print cotton decorator fabric, 54 inches (137.2 cm) wide

BACKING:

2¾ yards (2.5 m) of solid color cotton fabric, 90 inches (228.6 cm) wide

BINDING:

½ yard (0.5 m) of a small-scale circle print cotton fabric, 45 inches (114.3 cm) wide

BATTING:

Low-loft batting, 94 x 76 inches (238.8 x 193 cm)

THREAD, ETC:

Five assorted colors of embroidery floss

Sewing thread to blend with the decorator fabrics

TOOLS

Embroidery needle with a large eye

½-inch (6 mm) seam allowance

WILD ZEBRA

WENDI GRATZ

DESIGNER

You'll be surprised at the simple method you can use to sew the intricate-looking stripes on this graphic quilt. The arrangement of the blocks automatically creates contrasting stripes with jagged edges.

Finished size: approximately 88 x 61 inches (223.5 x 154.9 cm)

MATERIALS

BLOCKS:

A total of 6½ yards (5.9 m) of at least 10 assorted black print fabrics, 44 inches (111.8 cm) wide

A total of 2¾ yards (2.5 m) of at least 10 assorted white print fabrics, 44 inches (111.8 cm) wide

BACKING AND BINDING:

5½ yards (5 m) of black print fabric, 44 inches (111.8 cm) wide

BATTING:

Low-loft batting, 92 x 65 inches (233.7 x 165.1 cm)

THREAD:

Black and white sewing threads

TOOLS

4-inch (10.2 cm) square transparent ruler

¼-inch (6 mm) seam allowance

DESIGNER'S NOTE: For this quilt, you'll need many tone-on-tone fabric prints that are similar in value. For example, the assorted black prints range from very dark gray to deep black. They blend because they're in the same color family. Textured fabrics, such as jacquard weaves, corduroy, linen, and satin, can be used to add interest to each tonal mix.

INSTRUCTIONS

1 Use a rotary cutter to cut the assorted black print fabrics into about 625 strips 9 inches (22.9 cm) long by 1½ to 2 inches (3.8 to 5.1 cm) wide. You can be casual about measuring, because some of the strips should be wider at one end than the other. It's important for the edges of the strips to be straight, but they need not be parallel. In the same way, cut the assorted white print fabrics into exactly 250 strips.

2 Sew two black strips to each white strip with right sides together (see figure 1). Press the seams away from the white strip.

3 Use the square transparent ruler and a rotary cutter to cut two 4-inch (10.2 cm) square blocks from each set of pieced strips (see figure 2). Each block should appear as if it's black with a white stripe along one edge. If a pieced section is not large enough to cut two squares, sew a fourth black strip along one edge to enlarge it.

4 Sew the blocks into 20 rows of 25 blocks each, with the white stripe of each block facing the same direction (see figure 3). Press the seams to one side.

5 Sew each pair of rows together so the white stripes meet (see figure 4). Press the seams to one side.

6 Sew the rows together to complete the quilt top. Press the seams to one side.

7 Cut eight 1-inch (2.5 cm) crosswise strips from the black print fabric and reserve for the binding. Cut the remaining fabric crosswise into two equal sections measuring 95 inches (241.3 cm) to make the backing. Sew these sections with right sides together along a lengthwise edge. Press the seam open. Trim the backing to 93 x 66 inches (236.2 x 167.6 cm) with the seam centered.

8 Stack and baste the quilt layers.

9 Adjust the sewing machine for straight-stitch quilting. Thread the needle and fill the bobbin with white thread. Stitch a wavy line through the center of each white stripe. Thread the needle and fill the bobbin with black thread. Stitch two wavy lines near the center of each black stripe.

10 Bind the quilt, using a ¼-inch (6 mm) seam allowance and mitered corners.

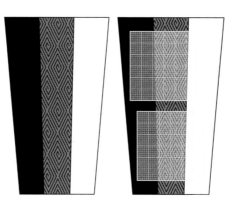

Figure 1   *Figure 2*

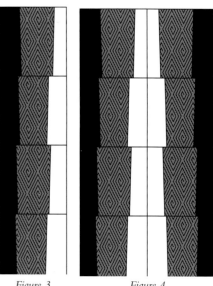

Figure 3   *Figure 4*

FOR BABY

SHARI LIDJI

DESIGNER

This cuddly crib quilt has plenty of contemporary style thanks to the fabric mix. Luxurious sateens like those used in finest-quality men's shirts produce a quilt that's soft as a baby's skin, while hand embroidery guarantees this piece will be treasured as a keepsake.

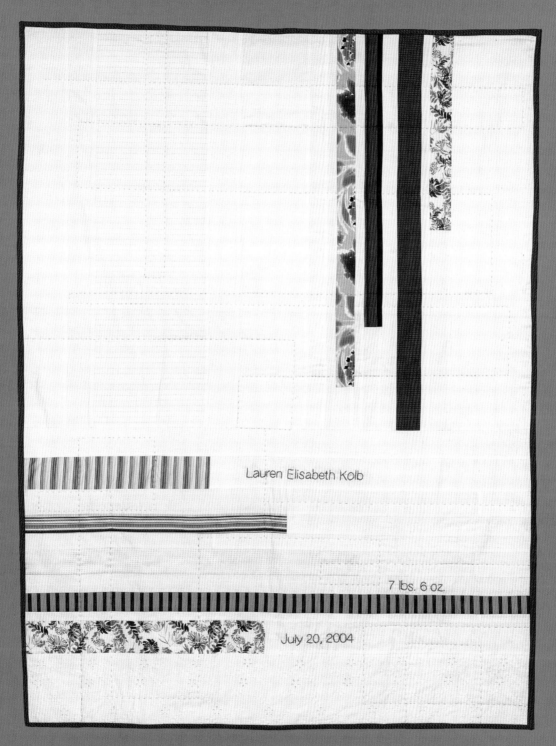

Lauren Elisabeth Kolb

7 lbs. 6 oz.

July 20, 2004

Finished size: approximately 54 x 41 inches (137.2 x 104.1 cm)

¼ yard (0.2 m) each of eight assorted white and off-white print cotton fabrics, 45 inches (114.3 cm) wide

⅜ yard (0.3 m) of one white or off-white print cotton fabric, 45 inches (114.3 cm) wide

¼ yard (0.2 m) of white cotton eyelet fabric, 45 inches (114.3 cm) wide

¼ yard (0.2 m) each of three pink floral-print cotton fabrics, 45 inches (114.3 cm) wide

¼ yard (0.2 m) each of three pink-striped cotton fabrics, 45 inches (114.3 cm) wide

BACKING:

1¾ yards (1.6 m) of pink floral-print cotton fabric, 45 inches (114.3 cm) wide

BINDING:

¼ yard (0.2 m) of pink print cotton fabric, 45 inches (114.3 cm) wide

BATTING:

Low-loft batting, 58 x 45 inches (147.3 x 114.3 cm)

THREAD ETC:

White sewing thread

Pink waxed cotton quilting thread

Pink perle cotton

TOOLS

Embroidery needle with a large eye

¼-inch (6 mm) seam allowance

DESIGNER'S NOTE: Most of the fabrics used to piece the quilt top are white and off-white prints. It's the accent strips cut from bright floral and striped prints that give the quilt a modern punch. For interest, some of the strips are pieced from two fabrics, while others are cut from a single fabric.

INSTRUCTIONS

1 Use a rotary cutter to cut fabric strips to size for the vertically-pieced section (see figure 1) and the horizontally-pieced section (see figure 2 on page 64). Begin by cutting the 10¾ x 31½ (27.3 x 80 cm) strip from the ⅜ yard (0.3m) of white or off-white fabric. Next, cut the accent strips from the pink floral-print and striped fabrics. Cut the remaining strips from the assorted white and off-white print fabrics.

2 Sew the pieces for each two-part strip with right sides together. Press the seams to one side.

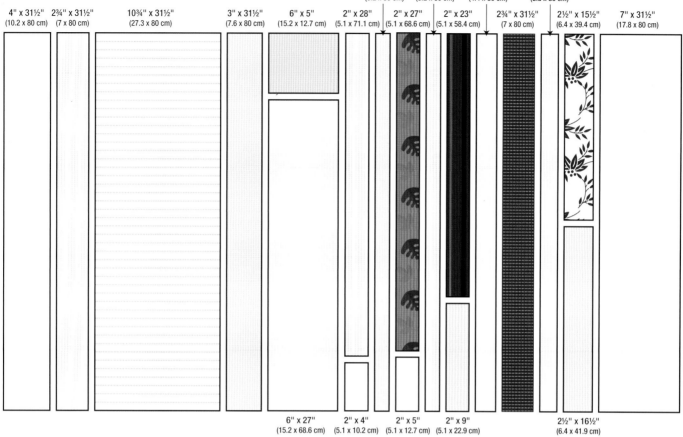

| 4" x 31½"
(10.2 x 80 cm) | 2¾" x 31½"
(7 x 80 cm) | 10¾" x 31½"
(27.3 x 80 cm) | 3" x 31½"
(7.6 x 80 cm) | 6" x 5"
(15.2 x 12.7 cm) | 2" x 28"
(5.1 x 71.1 cm) | 1¼" x 31½"
(3.2 x 80 cm) | 2" x 27"
(5.1 x 68.6 cm) | 1¼" x 31½"
(3.2 x 80 cm) | 2" x 23"
(5.1 x 58.4 cm) | 1¾" x 31½"
(4.4 x 80 cm) | 2¾" x 31½"
(7 x 80 cm) | 1½" x 31½"
(3.8 x 80 cm) | 2½" x 15½"
(6.4 x 39.4 cm) | 7" x 31½"
(17.8 x 80 cm) |

6" x 27"
(15.2 x 68.6 cm)

2" x 4"
(5.1 x 10.2 cm)

2" x 5"
(5.1 x 12.7 cm)

2" x 9"
(5.1 x 22.9 cm)

2½" x 16½"
(6.4 x 41.9 cm)

Figure 1

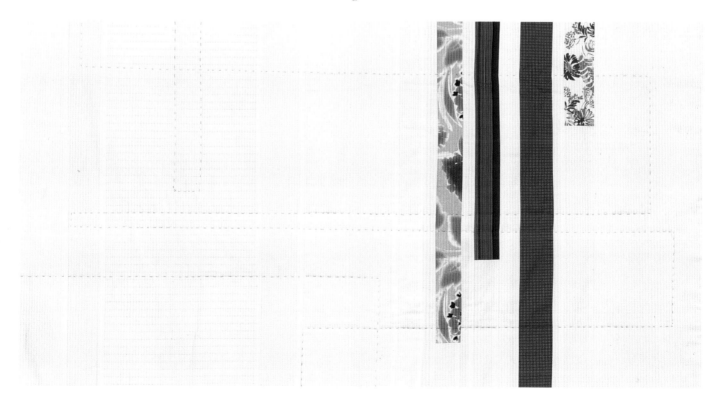

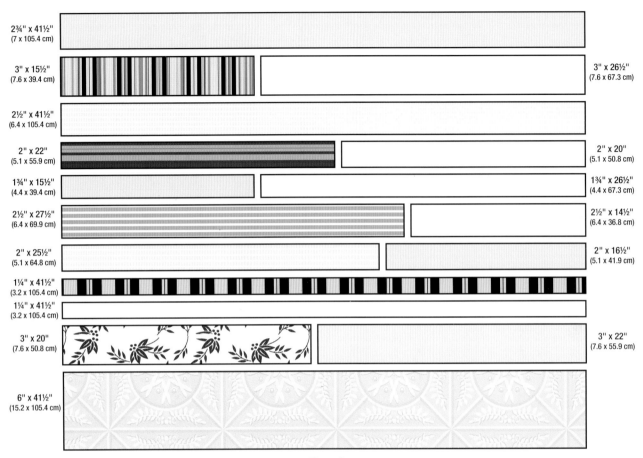

2¾" x 41½"
(7 x 105.4 cm)

3" x 15½"
(7.6 x 39.4 cm)

3" x 26½"
(7.6 x 67.3 cm)

2½" x 41½"
(6.4 x 105.4 cm)

2" x 22"
(5.1 x 55.9 cm)

2" x 20"
(5.1 x 50.8 cm)

1¾" x 15½"
(4.4 x 39.4 cm)

1¾" x 26½"
(4.4 x 67.3 cm)

2½" x 27½"
(6.4 x 69.9 cm)

2½" x 14½"
(6.4 x 36.8 cm)

2" x 25½"
(5.1 x 64.8 cm)

2" x 16½"
(5.1 x 41.9 cm)

1¼" x 41½"
(3.2 x 105.4 cm)

1¼" x 41½"
(3.2 x 105.4 cm)

3" x 20"
(7.6 x 50.8 cm)

3" x 22"
(7.6 x 55.9 cm)

6" x 41½"
(15.2 x 105.4 cm)

Figure 2

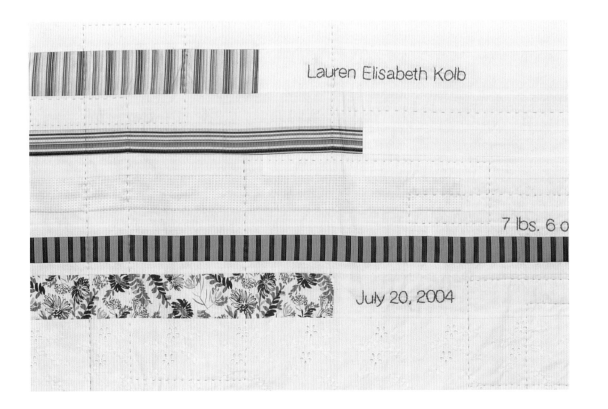

Lauren Elisabeth Kolb

7 lbs. 6 o

July 20, 2004

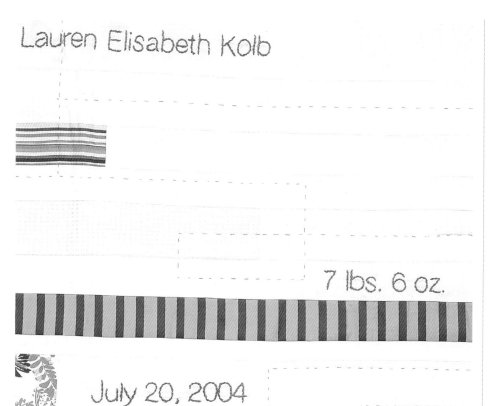

Lauren Elisabeth Kolb

7 lbs. 6 oz.

July 20, 2004

7 Thread a needle with waxed quilting thread. Quilt with running stitches. Sew the stitches in a pattern like stair steps (see figure 4) by sewing straight lines of running stitches horizontally across the quilt part of the way, then quilting in a straight line vertically for several inches before resuming quilting in a straight horizontal line across the quilt. Rectangular boxes will form where the stair steps intersect. Space the lines of quilting about 4 to 6 inches (10.2 to 15.2 cm) apart across the entire quilt.

8 Cut 1-inch (2.5 cm) crosswise strips from the binding fabric. Bind the quilt, using a ¼-inch (6 mm) seam allowance and mitered corners.

3 Sew the strips for each section with right sides together. Press the seams to one side.

4 Sew the two sections with right sides together. Press the seam toward the horizontally-pieced section.

5 Thread the embroidery needle with perle cotton. Use a stem stitch (see figure 3) to embroider the baby's name on one horizontal strip, the birth weight on another horizontal strip, and the birth date on a third horizontal strip.

6 Stack and baste the quilt layers.

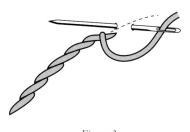

Figure 3

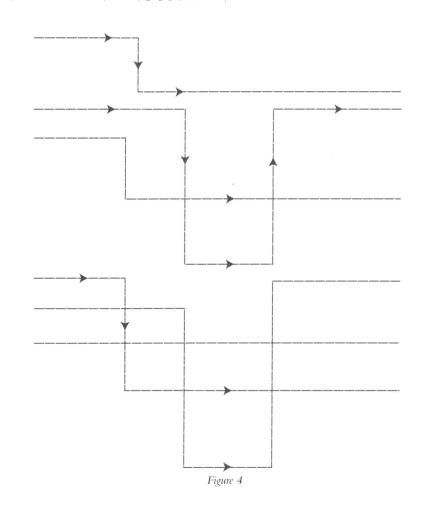

Figure 4

ZOE'S DEEP BLUE

JOAN K. MORRIS

DESIGNER

This quilt looks complex, but you simply vary the arrangement of three colors of fabrics among three geometric blocks to piece the quilt top. For the backing, sew four blue and green fabric rectangles together so the reverse relates to the quilt top with its own geometric theme.

Finished size: approximately 68 x 48 inches (172.7 x 121.9 cm)

MATERIALS

QUILT TOP, BACKING, AND BINDING:

4 yards (3.7 m) of light blue
sueded cotton fabric,
44 inches (111.8 cm) wide

3 yards (2.7 m) of green
sueded cotton fabric,
44 inches (111.8 cm) wide

1 yard 0(.9 m) of dark blue
sueded cotton fabric,
44 inches (111.8 cm) wide

BATTING:

Low-loft batting, 72 x 52 inches
(182.9 x 132.1 cm)

THREAD:

Light blue sewing thread

¼-inch (6 mm) seam allowance

DESIGNER'S NOTE: Sueded cotton
fabric is available in families of
graduated colors that are perfect
for this type of quilt design. It's
easy to change the quilt's color
scheme—just use fabrics from a
different graduated group.

INSTRUCTIONS

1 Cut two 37 x 27-inch (94 x 68.6 cm)
sections each from the light blue
and green fabrics, and reserve them for
the backing. Also cut six 2-inch (5.1 cm)
strips crosswise from green fabric, and
reserve them for the binding.

2 Follow the diagrams (see figures
1–6) to cut the remaining light blue,
dark blue, and green fabrics into strips to
piece blocks 1, 2, and 3. There are two
color schemes for each block; cut four
sets of strips for each color scheme.
Most of the time, you can simply cut the
fabrics into 1¼-, 1½-, and 2½-inch (3.2,
3.8, and 6.4 cm) crosswise strips, and
trim them to the length you need for each
block. Notice the outermost pieces of
each block are cut from light blue fabric.

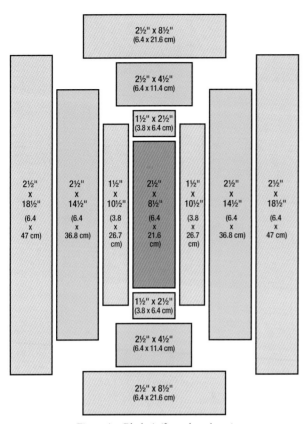

Figure 1 - Block 1 (first color scheme)

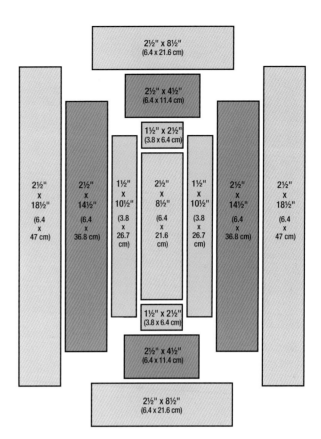

Figure 2 - Block 1 (second color scheme)

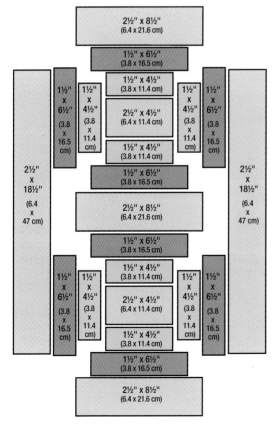

Figure 3 - Block 2 (first color scheme)

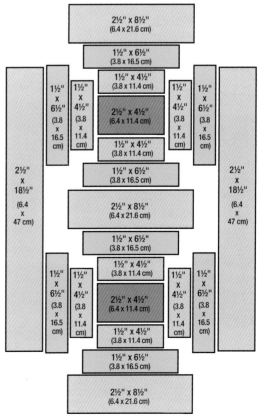

Figure 4- Block 2 (second color scheme)

69

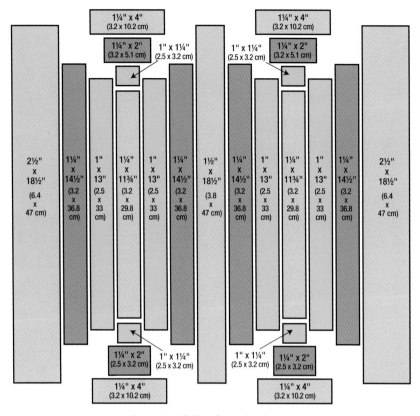

Figure 5 - Block 3 (fiirst color scheme)

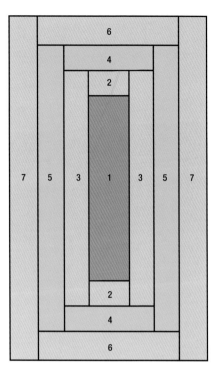

Figure 7

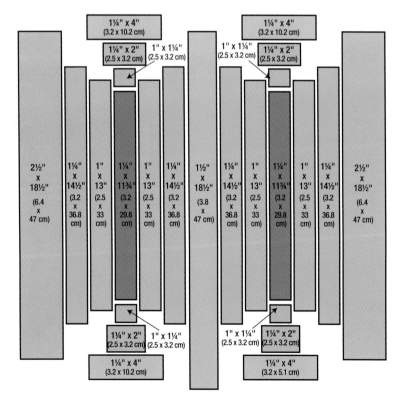

Figure 6 - Block 3 (second color scheme)

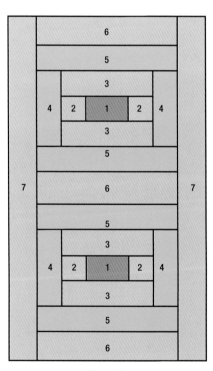

Figure 8

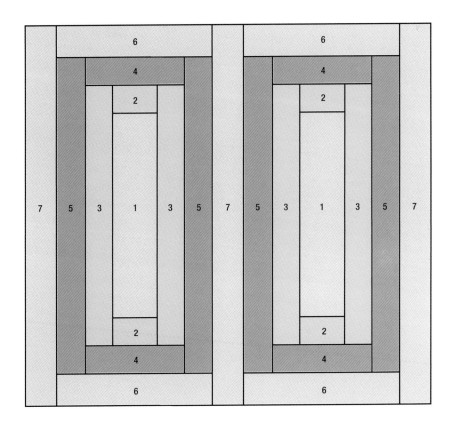

Figure 9

6 Stack and baste the quilt layers.

7 Adjust the sewing machine for straight-stitch quilting and stitch a quilting design of diamonds. Space the rows of stitches 2 inches (5.1 cm) apart.

8 Bind the quilt, using a ½-inch (1.3 cm) seam allowance and butted corners.

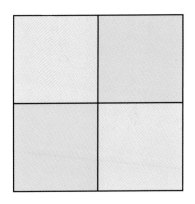

Figure 10

3 Stitch each block from the center out to the edges following the sequence shown in figure 7 for Block 1; in figure 8 for Block 2; and in figure 9 for Block 3. As you complete the stitching of each pair of seams, press the seams away from the center of the block.

4 Stitch the blocks into rows, arranging them as in the photo on page 67. Press the seams to one sid.

5 Stitch the longer edges of each pair of reserved light blue and green backing sections with right sides together. Press the seams toward the green sections. Stitch these sections with right sides together so the colors contrast (see figure 10). Press this seam open.

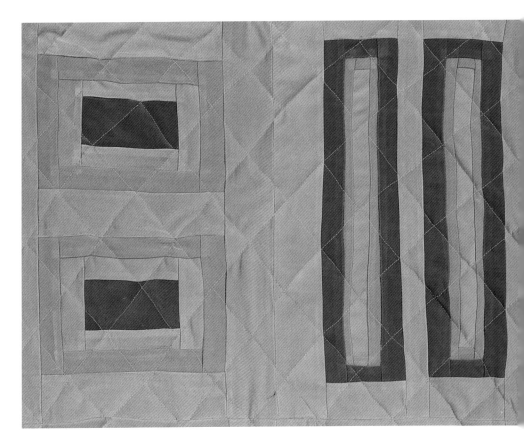

MARTINI DOT

JOAN K. MORRIS

DESIGNER

Rows of imaginary martinis, complete with olive garnish, adorn this puffy throw made from sandwashed silks. The basic blocks are simple squares with crisscross tucks stitched through the center to create the impression of more intricate seaming.

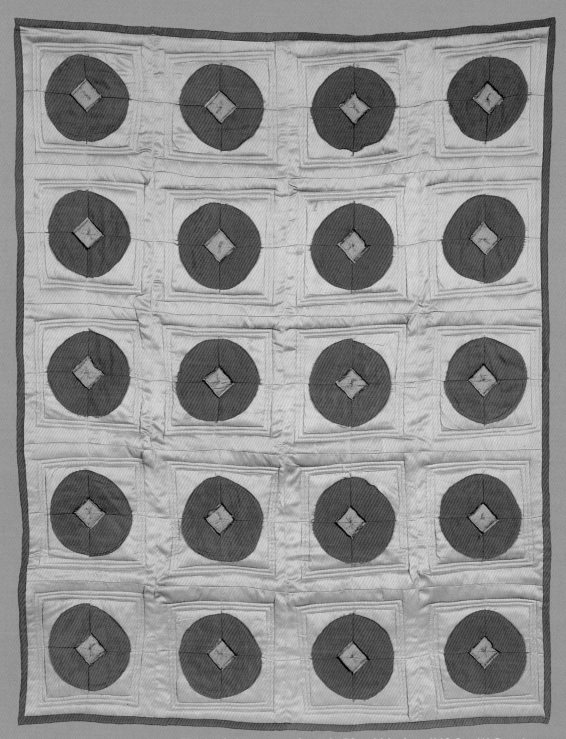

Finished size: approximately 56 x 44 inches (142.2 x 111.8 cm)

MATERIALS

BLOCKS:

2⅝ yards (2.4 m) of gold sandwashed silk fabric, 44 inches (111.8 cm) wide

BACKING, BINDING, & APPLIQUÉS:

3 yards (2.7 m) of purple sandwashed silk fabric, 44 inches (111.8 cm) wide

⅛ yard (0.1 m) of turquoise silk dupioni fabric, 44 inches (111.8 cm) wide

BATTING:

High-loft batting, 60 x 48 inches (152.4 x 121.9 cm)

THREAD, ETC:

Purple and gold sewing threads

Clear nylon thread

1 skein of gold embroidery floss

TOOLS & SUPPLIES

Plate or bowl 8 inches (20.3 cm) in diameter

Freezer paper

Fabric glue stick

Chalk fabric marker

Quilter's spray adhesive

Embroidery needle with a large eye

¼-inch (6 mm) seam allowance

DESIGNER'S NOTE: Because sandwashed silk fabrics can be slick and slippery to handle, this project uses helpful supplies such as freezer paper, glue stick, and spray adhesive for better control.

INSTRUCTIONS

1 Cut a backing 56 inches (142.2 cm) long from purple fabric, and reserve. Cut five 2-inch (5.1 cm) crosswise strips from purple fabric, and reserve them for the binding. Use the remaining purple fabric for the martini appliqués.

2 Use chalk fabric marker to trace the plate or bowl outline 20 times onto the matte side of freezer paper to make the martini appliqué patterns. Cut apart the patterns roughly, leaving a margin of paper around each traced circle.

3 Press the shiny side of each pattern onto the wrong side of the remaining purple fabric using a dry iron. Cut out each martini appliqué on the traced outline.

4 Cut twenty 13-inch (33 cm) squares of gold fabric for the quilt blocks.

5 Apply glue stick around the edge of each martini appliqué as you peel off the freezer paper to arrange an appliqué in the center of each gold block.

6 Adjust the sewing machine for raw-edge appliqué with a straight stitch. Thread the needle with clear nylon thread and fill the bobbin with purple thread. Stitch each martini appliqué in place.

7 Fold each block in half with right sides together. Thread the needle and fill the bobbin with gold thread. Stitch as closely as possible to the fold, creating a tiny tuck. Open out the block, fold it in half in the other direction, and stitch another tuck in the same way. Open out the block and press the tucks to one side so the block is flat.

8 Stitch the blocks into five rows of four blocks each. Press the seams open. Stitch the rows together to make the quilt top. Press the seams open.

9 Cut a 9-inch (22.9 cm) square from freezer paper. Use a dry iron to position the square temporarily in the center of each block and chalk-mark a quilting guideline in each block.

10 Cut twenty 2-inch (5.1 cm) square appliqués from turquoise fabric. Use the glue stick to place an appliqué in the center of each block; align the appliqué corners with the tucks on the blocks.

11 Spray one side of the batting with adhesive. Smooth the quilt backing right side up over the batting, with an even margin of batting extending all around. Flip the layers so the batting is on top. Spray the other side of the batting with adhesive. Arrange the quilt top right side up smoothly and evenly over the batting, aligning the quilt top with the backing. Use safety pins to baste the layers together at the corners of each block.

12 Adjust the sewing machine for straight-stitch quilting. Work from the center of the quilt out toward the edges. Stitch a scant ¼ inch (6 mm) in from the raw edge of each turquoise appliqué; backstitch to lock the stitches at the end. Stitch on the 9-inch (22.9 cm) square quilting guideline marked on each block, backstitching to lock the stitches at the end. In the same way, stitch a second square ¼ inch (6 mm) outside the first, and a third square ¼ inch (6 mm) outside the second.

13 Thread the embroidery needle with six strands of floss. Tie the quilt in the center of each turquoise appliqué.

14 Trim the quilt so the edges of the layers are even and the corners are square. Bind the quilt, using a ½-inch (1.3 cm) seam allowance and butted corners.

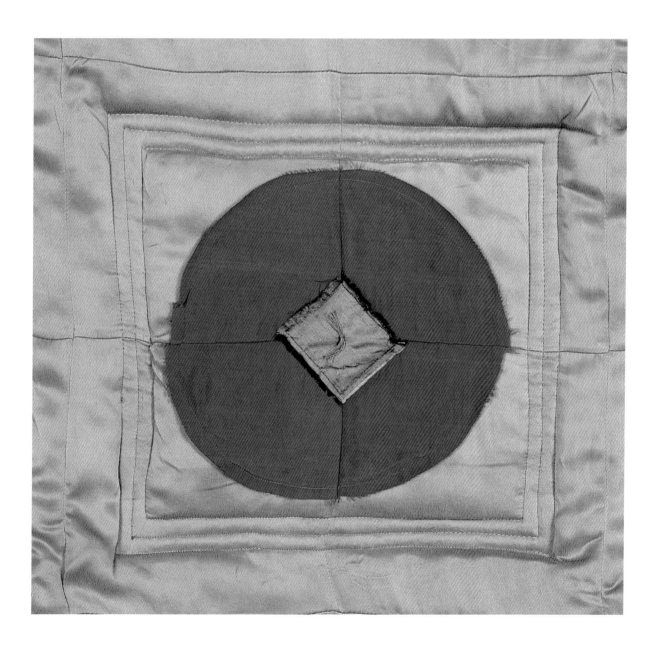

DANCING
SQUARES

WENDI GRATZ

DESIGNER

The yellow squares on this queen-sized quilt are easier to make than they look, and they add a sense of movement to this lively project. The final design emerges after you cut the initial sections into simple squares and arrange the squares into blocks.

Finished size: approximately 88 inches (223.5 cm) square

MATERIALS

BLOCKS:

A total of 11¼ yards (10.3 m) of at least 10 assorted red print fabrics, 44 inches (111.8 cm) wide

A total of 1 yard (0.9 m) of at least six assorted yellow print fabrics, 44 inches (111.8 cm) wide

Scraps of at least four lavender print fabrics

BACKING AND BINDING:

8½ yards (7.8 m) of red print fabric, 44 inches (111.8 cm) wide

BATTING:

Low-loft batting, 95½ inches (242.6 cm) square

THREAD:

Red sewing thread

TOOLS

4-inch (10.2 cm) square transparent ruler

¼-inch (6 mm) seam allowance

DESIGNER'S NOTE: You'll need many red print fabrics to create this quilt. Choose dark reds ranging from almost orange to brick; the colors will blend together even though they don't match. Add textured fabrics such as corduroy, linen, jacquard weave, or satin to the tonal mix for extra visual interest.

INSTRUCTIONS

1 Use a rotary cutter to cut the assorted red print fabrics into about 1,083 strips 9 x 1½ to 2 inches (22.9 x 3.8 to 5.1 cm). Don't be too fussy about the measurements; in fact, some of the strips should be wider at one end than the other. It's important for the edges of the strips to be straight, but they don't have to be parallel. In the same way, cut the assorted yellow print fabrics into exactly 96 strips and the lavender scraps into four strips, each of which is also 9 x 1½ to 2 inches (22.9 x 3.8 to 5.1 cm).

2 Sew three red strips together to make 238 pieced sections (see figure 1), sew two red strips and one

Figure 1

Figure 2

yellow strip together to make 96 pieced sections (see figure 2), and sew two red strips and one lavender strip together to make four pieced sections (see figure 3). Press the seams to one side.

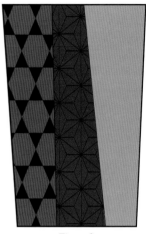

Figure 3

3 Use the square transparent ruler and a rotary cutter to cut two 4-inch (10.2 cm) squares from each pieced section. Try to place the ruler so each two-color pieced section yields a contrasting stripe at an angle along one edge (see figure 4). If a pieced section is not large enough to cut two squares, sew a fourth red strip along one edge to enlarge the section.

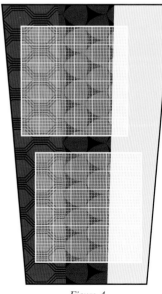

Figure 4

4 Sew together eight red squares and eight red/yellow squares to make each of 12 "A" blocks (see figure 5). Also sew together eight red squares and eight red/lavender squares to make one "A" block. Sew together eight red squares and eight red/yellow squares to make each of 12 "B" blocks (see figure 6). Press the seams to one side.

Figure 5: Block A

Figure 6: Block B

5 Refer to figure 7 on page 80 for steps 5 and 6. Sew together four red squares to make each of 30 "C" sashing strips. As you sew the squares together, arrange them so the pieced strips are oriented alternately horizontally and vertically. Press the seams to one side. In the same way, sew together 25 red squares to make each of six "D" sashing strips.

6 Sew the blocks and "C" sashing strips together to make each row, alternating the "A" and "B" blocks as shown in figure 7. Press the seams to one side. Sew the rows together with a "D" sashing strip in between to complete the quilt top. Press the seams to one side.

7 Cut ten 1-inch (2.5 cm) crosswise strips from the red print fabric and reserve for the binding. Cut the remaining fabric crosswise into three equal sections to make the backing; each section should be 98½ inches (250.2 cm) long. Sew these sections with right sides together along a lengthwise edge. Press the seams open. Trim to 96½ inches (245.1 cm) square.

8 Stack and baste the quilt layers.

9 Adjust the sewing machine for straight-stitch quilting. Thread the needle and fill the bobbin with red thread. Stitch a diagonal grid over the entire quilt, guiding the needle by eye from one corner of a square to the corner diagonally opposite

10 Bind the quilt, using a ¼-inch (6 mm) seam allowance and mitered corners.

A Block B Block   D Sashing Strip

C Sashing Str

Figure 7

FLOWERS

JUDE STUECKER

DESIGNER

It's easy to sew the creative touches that make this quilt bloom. Piece the quilt top from simple strips, and topstitch rows of ribbon and rickrack here and there to add detail. Enhance a trio of bright pink flower appliqués with satin stitching and free-motion quilting.

Finished size: approximately 84 x 57 inches (213.4 x 144.8 cm)

⅜ yard (0.3 m) each of eight green print fabrics, 45 inches wide (114.3 cm)

2¼ yards (2.1 m) each of three to five assorted flat trims such as grosgrain ribbon and rickrack

APPLIQUÉS:

¼ yard (0.2 m) each of four pink print fabrics for the flower petals, 45 inches wide (114.3 cm)

¼ yard (0.2 m) of dark pink fabric for the flower centers, 45 inches wide (114.3 cm)

2⅝ yards (2.4 m) of paper-backed fusible web, 17 inches (43.2 cm) wide

BORDERS:

½ yard (0.5 m) of light pink print fabric for the inner border, 45 inches wide (114.3 cm)

¾ yard (0.7 m) of medium pink print fabric for the outer border, 45 inches wide (114.3 cm)

BACKING:

5 yards (4.6 m) of green fabric, 45 inches wide (114.3 cm)

BINDING:

⅜ yard (0.3 m) of striped fabric, 45 inches wide (114.3 cm)

BATTING:

Low-loft batting, 88 x 61 inches (223.5 x 154.9 cm)

THREAD:

Pink and green sewing threads

TEMPLATES:

See page 123

¼-inch (6 mm) seam allowance

84

DESIGNER'S NOTE: Hand-dyed cotton batik fabrics, distinctive for their mottled colors and tone-on-tone print motifs, add depth and intensity to the floral appliqués.

INSTRUCTIONS

1 Cut each green print fabric in half crosswise to make two pieces that are each 6¾ x 45 inches (17.1 x 114.3 cm) long. Sew the short ends with right sides together to create one long strip from each green print fabric. Press the seams open.

2 Cut each green fabric strip so it measures 79½ inches (201.9 cm) long, staggering the cuts so the seams do not fall at the same place on any of the eight strips.

3 Use a rotary cutter to cut each green fabric strip into strips of various widths from about 3 to 6 inches (7.6 to 15.2 cm).

4 Thread the sewing machine needle and fill the bobbin with green thread. Stitch the long edges of the strips with right sides together to create a quilt top 52½ inches (133.4 cm) wide. Press the seams open.

5 Topstitch the flat trims on some of the strips on the quilt top.

6 Make fusible appliqués by tracing the following templates: 27 of Template A and three of Template B.

7 Arrange the appliqués, right side up, to make three flowers on the quilt top. Remove the paper backing from each appliqué, and fuse following the manufacturer's directions.

8 Adjust the sewing machine for satin-stitch appliqué. Thread the needle and fill the bobbin with pink thread. Stitch around the edge of each appliqué.

9 Cut the light pink fabric crosswise into 2½ x 45-inch (6.4 x 114.3 cm) strips for the inner border and the medium pink fabric crosswise into 3½ x 45-inch (8.9 x 114.3 cm) strips for the outer border. Attach the borders.

10 Cut the backing fabric in half crosswise so each piece measures 2½ yards (2.3 m) long. Sew the halves with right sides together along one long edge. Press the seam open. Trim the backing to 89 x 62 inches (226.1 x 157.5 cm).

11 Stack and baste the quilt layers.

12 Adjust the sewing machine for straight-stitch quilting. Thread the needle and fill the bobbin with green thread. Stitch ¼ inch (6 mm) from each side of the seams of the strips on the quilt top. Thread the needle with pink thread. Stitch in the ditch of each border seam.

13 Adjust the sewing machine for free-motion quilting. Stitch within each petal to echo the outline of the appliqué. Stitch swirls within each flower center.

14 Cut 1 x 45-inch (2.5 x 114.3 cm) strips crosswise from the striped fabric. Bind the quilt, using a ¼-inch (6 mm) seam allowance and mitered corners.

CROP CIRCLES

JEN SWEARINGTON

DESIGNER

The beauty of this silk shantung throw comes from circle appliqués cut free-hand to create an organic look. Stitch the quilted furrows casually for a soft, undulating effect. A bit of hand embroidery adds texture, detail, and a shot of color.

Finished size: approximately 60 x 44 inches (152.4 x 111.8 cm)

3⅝ yards (3.3 m) of orange silk shantung, 54 inches (137.2 cm) wide

APPLIQUÉS:

1 yard (0.9 m) each of pink velvet and pink corduroy, 45 inches (114.3 cm) wide

½ yard (0.5 m) of white silk organza, 42 inches (106.7 cm) wide

BINDING:

½ yard (0.5 m) of red silk fabric, 45 inches (114.3 cm) wide

BATTING:

Low-loft cotton batting, 64 x 48 inches (162.6 x 121.9 cm)

THREAD, ETC:

Red sewing thread

Neutral sewing thread to blend with the orange shantung

Black heavy-duty cotton/polyester thread

Clear monofilament nylon thread

Bulky red acrylic yarn

TOOLS

Embroidery needle with a large eye

Two rulers or other long straight-edge tools

¼-inch (6 mm) seam allowance

INSTRUCTIONS

1 Trim the selvages off the orange silk shantung. Cut a quilt top 62 x 46 inches (157.5 x 116.8 cm) and a backing 65 x 49 inches (165.1 x 124.5 cm).

2 Cut the pink velvet and corduroy fabrics crosswise into 8-inch (20.3 cm) strips. With right sides together, sew the strips into a panel, alternating the velvet and corduroy strips. Press the seams open.

3 For the appliqués, cut 12 roughly circular rings 12 inches (30.5 cm) in diameter and 2 to 3 inches (5.1 to 7.6 cm) thick from the pieced velvet/corduroy panel. Stagger the cuts so the proportion of velvet to corduroy differs from one appliqué to another.

4 Arrange the appliqués on the right side of the quilt top in three rows of four appliqués each. Leave a border of about 6 inches (15.2 cm) all around the edge of the quilt top. Pin each appliqué in place.

5 Thread the sewing machine and fill the bobbin with red sewing thread. Zigzag stitch the raw-edge appliqués. Stitch the outer and inner edges of each appliqué.

6 Place a ruler or other straight edge diagonally through the center of each pair of appliqués to find the midpoint of the space in between (see figure 1). Mark each midpoint with a pin.

7 Thread the embroidery needle with red yarn. To embroider a cross at each midpoint, knot the end of the yarn and bring the needle through to the right side at the midpoint mark. Sew running stitches about ¼ inch (6 mm) long for 2½ to 3 inches (6.4 to 7.6 cm), then return to the midpoint by sewing running stitches in between the first set, filling in the arm of the cross. Sew the remaining three arms of each cross the same way (figure 2). Secure the yarn on the wrong side with a knot.

8 Trim the quilt top to 60 x 44 inches (152.4 x 111.8 cm). Stack and baste the quilt layers.

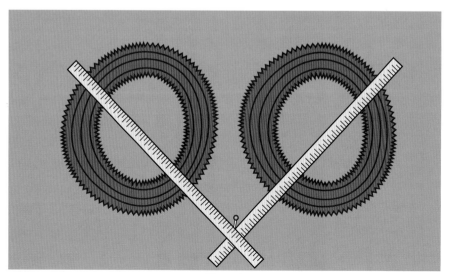

Figure 1

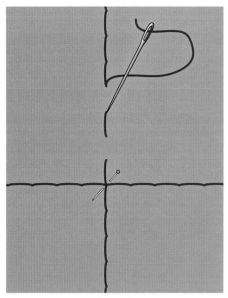

Figure 2

9 Thread the sewing machine needle with black heavy-duty thread and fill the bobbin with neutral thread. Adjust the machine for straight-stitch quilting. Stitch horizontally and vertically through the center of the appliqués to form a grid over the entire quilt. Stitch diagonally through the center of the appliqués and the crosses to form a second grid.

10 Repeat step 9, using the previously stitched grids as a guide but deviating slightly from them to make the lines of black stitches more visible.

11 Thread the sewing machine needle with red thread. Stitch horizontally and vertically through the arms of the embroidered crosses to form a grid over the entire quilt. As you reach each embroidered arm, adjust the machine for a short, narrow zigzag stitch to couch the yarn securely. Return to straight stitching in between the crosses.

12 Adjust the sewing machine for free-motion quilting. Stitch several concentric circles on each appliqué.

13 Cut one rough circle about 18 inches (45.7 cm) in diameter from the white organza fabric. Cut one rough circle about 14 inches (35.6 cm) in diameter from the center of the first circle; in the same way, cut one rough circle about 11 inches (27.9 cm) in diameter, then one 8 inches (20.3 cm) in diameter from the centers. Use the three larger circles for appliqués. (Recycle the 8-inch [20.3 cm] circle.)

14 Arrange the white organza appliqués on the quilt top, and pin them in place.

15 Adjust the sewing machine for zigzag stitching. Thread the needle with clear nylon thread. Zigzag the outer and inner edges of each white organza raw-edge appliqué.

16 Adjust the machine for free-motion quilting. Stitch a few concentric circles on each white organza appliqué.

17 Use a rotary cutter to cut 1½-inch (3.8 cm) strips crosswise from the red fabric. Bind the quilt using a ¼-inch seam allowance and making a double-layer binding with mitered corners.

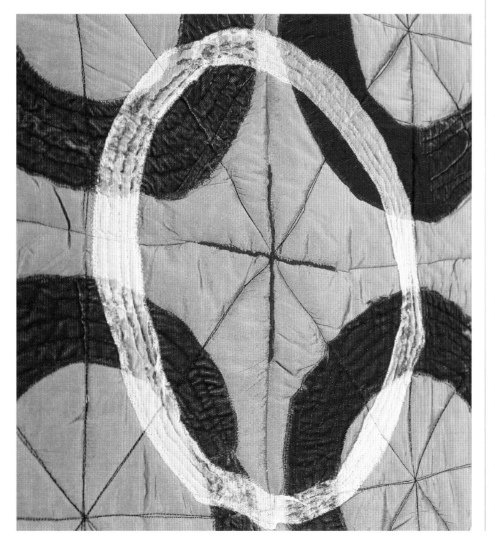

SEA MOODS

DIANNE FIRTH

DESIGNER

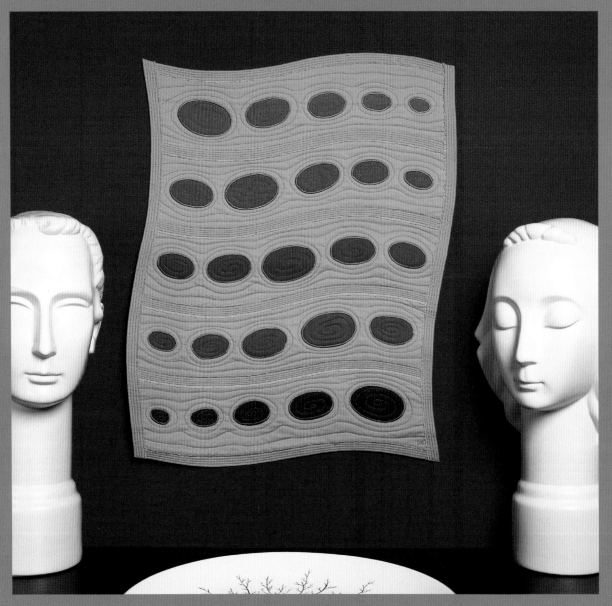

This unconventional art quilt calls for tearing fabric into crosswise strips, then pressing them into fluid curves. Leave the soft fringe on the torn edges to add texture and detail. For the bubbles on this sea-themed quilt, appliqué rows of ovals in graduated sizes.

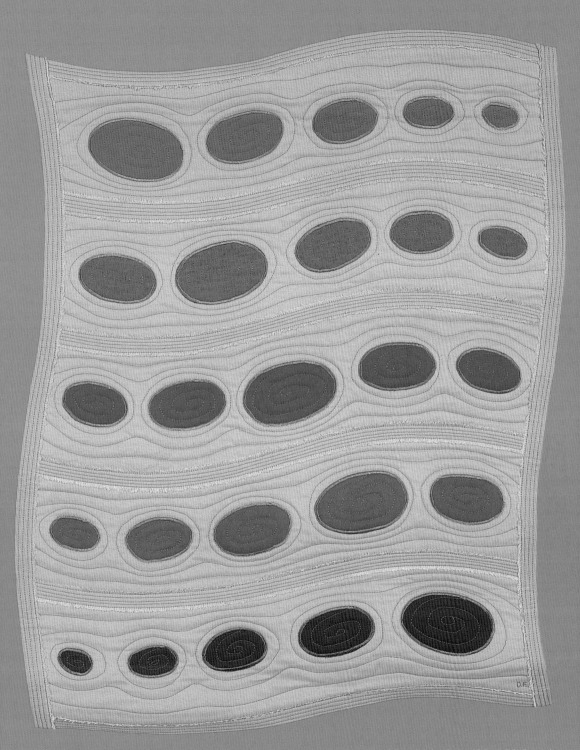

Finished Size: approximately 26 x 20 inches (66 x 50.8 cm)

QUILT TOP, WAVE APPLIQUÉS, AND BINDING:

1 yard (0.9 m) of solid color cotton fabric, 45 inches (114.3 cm) wide

OVAL APPLIQUÉS:

Five 9-inch (22.9 cm) squares of solid color cotton fabrics

½ yard (0.5 m) of paper-backed fusible web, 17 inches (43.2 cm) wide

BACKING:

¾ yard (0.7 m) of cotton fabric, 45 inches (114.3 cm) wide

BATTING:

Low-loft polyester batting, 30 x 24 inches (76.2 x 61 cm)

THREAD, ETC:

Machine embroidery thread slightly darker than the quilt top fabric

Sewing thread to match the backing fabric

22-inch (55.9 cm) wood dowel, ¼ inch (6 mm) in diameter

TOOLS & SUPPLIES

Chalk fabric marker

Large piece of paper

TEMPLATES:

See page 124

INSTRUCTIONS

1 Tear two test strips ¾-inch (1.9 cm) wide crosswise from the quilt top fabric. Press one strip with a steam iron, pulling the strip gently under the iron to coax it to rise to a curve about ¾ inch (1.9 cm) high within the first 10 inches (25.4 cm) of the strip's length. In the same way, press a curve that dips to shape the strip into an "S" on its side (see figure 1). Trim the excess fabric from the strip to make the "S" curve 20 inches (50.8 cm) long. In a similar way, press the second strip into an "S" curve 26 inches (66 cm) long.

Figure 1

2 Pin each test strip to paper. Cut along the top of the shorter strip to create a paper pattern for the top and bottom edges of the quilt; this pattern will also be used to shape the wave appliqués. Cut along the top of the longer strip to create a paper pattern for the side edges of the quilt.

3 Tear three strips that are each ¾-inch (1.9 cm) wide. Cut them into five strips 20 inches (50.8 cm) long and reserve for the wave appliqués.

DESIGNER'S NOTE: A graduated palette of fabric colors is the key to this quilt. While blue, green, and purple gradations are used here to evoke water, other color combinations could reflect other themes. For example, you might choose brown, gold, and orange fabrics to establish a desert mood, imagining the curved strips are wind patterns on the sand and the ovals are pebbles.

4 Tear four strips crosswise from the quilt top fabric, each 1¾ inches (4.4 cm) wide, and reserve them for the binding. Cut the quilt top 28 x 22 inches (71.1 x 55.9 cm) from the remaining fabric. Use the paper patterns to cut curves along the edges of the quilt top.

5 Use a chalk fabric marker and the smaller paper pattern to draw four wave appliqué placement lines about 5 inches (12.7 cm) apart across the quilt top, beginning ½ inch (1.3 cm) from the top edge.

6 Use the smaller paper pattern to press the wave appliqués into curved shapes. Pin the appliqués to the placement lines marked on the quilt top.

7 Make fusible appliqués by tracing the following templates: two of Template A, four of Template B, six of Template C, seven of Template D, and five of Template E.

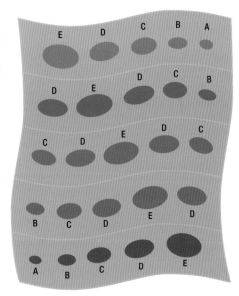

Figure 2

8 Follow the key (see figure 2) to fuse five ovals per wave to each 9-inch (22.9 cm) fabric square. Peel off the paper backings and fuse the appliqués to the quilt top following the manufacturer's directions.

9 Stack and baste the quilt layers.

10 Adjust the sewing machine for satin-stitch appliqué. Thread the needle with embroidery thread and fill the bobbin with regular sewing thread. Stitch around the edge of each oval appliqué; adjust the sewing machine for straight stitching to continue stitching a spiral in the center of each oval.

11 Adjust the sewing machine for straight-stitch quilting. Stitch just inside each raw edge of each wave appliqué. Quilt three additional rows between the previous rows of stitches. Finally, quilt two curving lines in between each wave and oval appliqué and an oval outline around each oval appliqué.

12 Trim the batting and backing even with the quilt top. Reserve the excess backing fabric for a hanging sleeve.

13 Fold each reserved binding strip along its length, with wrong sides together, so one edge slightly extends beyond the other edge. Press the fold.

14 Use the paper patterns to press the binding strips into curved shapes to match the quilt edges. Fold a binding strip over the top and the bottom edges of the quilt, with the shorter portion of the strip on top. With the quilt top facing up, stitch through all layers just inside the raw edge of each binding strip. Stitch three more rows parallel to the first row of stitches on each binding strip. Trim the ends of each binding strip even with the quilt top. In the same way, stitch the binding strips to the side edges of the quilt, but turn under the raw edge 1/4 inch (6 mm) at each end.

15 Cut a 25 x 2½-inch (63.5 x 6.4 cm) hanging sleeve from the reserved backing fabric. Add the hanging sleeve. Insert the dowel into the sleeve to mount the quilt on the wall.

BROCADE
ON PARADE

JUDE STUECKER

DESIGNER

The focal point of this quilt is free-motion quilting stitched in a stipple motif. The quilt top is pieced simply from upholstery fabrics, but the generous quilting mimics the texture of luxurious brocade.

Finished size: approximately 87 x 81 inches (221 x 205.7 cm)

MATERIALS

SASHING:

2 yards (1.8 m) of fabric, 45 inches (114.3 cm) wide

BLOCKS:

⅔ yard (.6 m) each of seven different fabrics, 45 inches (114.3 cm) wide

BORDER:

1¼ yards (1.1 m) of fabric, 45 inches (114.3 cm) wide

BACKING AND BINDING:

6 yards (5.5 m) of fabric, 45 inches (114.3 cm) wide

BATTING:

Low-loft batting, 91 x 85 inches (231.1 x 215.9 cm)

THREAD:

Sewing thread to match each fabric

¼-inch (6 mm) seam allowance

INSTRUCTIONS

1 Cut the sashing fabric into 2½-inch (6.4 cm) crosswise strips. Sew the short ends with right sides together to make one, long strip. Press the seams open.

2 Cut the block fabrics into large rectangles of various sizes to create six rows of blocks. The rectangles should be from 8 to 16 inches (20.3 to 40.6 cm) wide and in various lengths so each row contains two, three, or four blocks.

3 Stitch the blocks into rows with a sashing strip in between the blocks, adjusting the length of the blocks if necessary so each row measures 70½ inches (179.1 cm) from one side edge to the other. (Before you begin stitching, you may find it helpful to overlap the blocks and sashing strips on the seamlines to test the length of the blocks.)

4 Stitch five of the rows together with a sashing strip in between each row. Trim the sashing strips even with the ends of the rows. Before stitching the final row in place, measure the quilt top. Including the final row, the quilt top should measure 78½ inches (199.4 cm) long; add a row or trim the final row if the size of the quilt top needs adjustment.

5 Stitch a sashing strip along each side edge of the quilt top, then along the top and bottom edges.

6 Cut the border fabric into crosswise strips 4½ inches (11.4 cm) wide. Attach the border.

7 Cut eight 1-inch (2.5 cm) strips crosswise from the fabric for the backing and binding, and reserve these strips for the binding. Cut the remaining fabric in half crosswise into two 104-inch (264.2 cm) pieces. Sew the pieces with right sides together along one lengthwise edge to make the backing. Press the seam open. Trim the backing so it measures 92 x 88 inches (233.7 x 223.5 cm) with the seam centered.

8 Stack and baste the quilt layers.

9 Adjust the sewing machine for free-motion quilting. Fill the bobbin with thread that matches the backing. Using thread that matches each section of the quilt top, stitch over the entire quilt in a stipple design—a continuous line of stitching that doesn't overlap (see figure 1).

10 Bind the quilt, using a ¼-inch (6 mm) seam allowance and mitered corners.

Figure 1

CONSTELLATIONS

JUDE STUECKER

DESIGNER

Surround the appliquéd stars on this heavenly quilt with circular orbits of free-motion quilting, and link the orbits into constellations with bold running stitches. The lightweight linen fabrics suggested for this design make a wonderfully soft and supple quilt.

Finished size: approximately 88 x 78 inches (223.5 x 198.1 cm)

MATERIALS

QUILT TOP:

4 yards (3.7 m) of medium blue lightweight linen fabric, 54 inches (137.2 cm) wide

APPLIQUÉS:

3⅛ yards (2.9 m) of paper-backed fusible web, 17 inches (43.2 cm) wide

1¼ (1.2 m) yards of white cotton fabric, 45 inches (114.3 cm) wide

BORDER:

⅜ yard (0.3 m) each of five assorted blue lightweight linen and linen-blend fabrics, 54 inches (137.2 cm) wide

BACKING:

6½ yards (5.9 m) of light blue lightweight linen fabric, 54 inches (137.2 cm) wide

BATTING:

Low-loft batting, 92 x 82 inches (233.7 x 208.3 cm)

BINDING:

½ yard (0.5 m) of dark blue lightweight linen fabric, 54 inches (137.2 cm) wide

THREAD, ETC.:

Blue and white sewing threads

2 skeins of white embroidery floss

TOOLS

Embroidery needle with a large eye

TEMPLATES

See page 125

¼-inch (6 mm) seam allowance

INSTRUCTIONS

1 Prewash all fabrics.

2 Cut two 66½-inch (168.9 cm) lengthwise panels of medium blue linen fabric for the quilt top. Cut one panel in half lengthwise to create two half-panels measuring 66½ x 27 inches (168.9 x 68.6 cm). Stitch each half-panel to the whole panel with right sides together. Press the seams open. Trim an equal amount from the long edge of each half-panel (see figure 1) so the quilt top background measures 76½ x 66½ inches (194.3 x 168.9 cm).

Figure 1

3 Make fusible appliqués by tracing the following star patterns: 10 of Template A, 10 of Template B, and 4 of Template C.

4 Arrange the appliqués, right side up, on the quilt top. Remove the paper backing from each appliqué, and fuse following the manufacturer's directions.

5 Adjust the sewing machine for satin-stitched appliqué, threading the needle and filling the bobbin with white thread. Stitch around the edge of each appliqué.

DESIGNER'S NOTE: The stars for the original quilt were cut from a vintage print drapery panel; you could substitute any fabric with a luster such as sateen or lamé.

You'll need to purchase a little extra lightweight linen fabric to accommodate the shrinkage that will occur during prewashing. The fabric quantities are generous to allow for this.

6 Cut the assorted blue linen border fabrics into crosswise strips 6½ inches (16.5 cm) wide. Cut the strips into assorted lengths of about 6 to 12 inches (15.2 to 30.5 cm). Attach the border.

7 Cut the light blue linen fabric in half crosswise to create two panels for the backing, each measuring 3¼ yards (3 m) long. Stitch the two panels together along the lengthwise edges. Press the seam open. Trim the quilt backing to 93 x 83 inches (236.2 x 210.8 cm) with the seam centered.

8 Stack and baste the quilt layers.

9 Adjust the sewing machine for straight-stitch quilting. Thread the needle with white thread and fill the bobbin with blue thread. Stitch along the inner edge of each appliqué, next to the satin stitching.

10 Adjust the sewing machine for free-motion quilting. Stitch six to eight tight circles around each appliqué to create orbits.

11 Adjust the sewing machine for straight-stitch quilting, threading the needle and filling the bobbin with blue thread. Stitch in the ditch of the border seam all around the edge of the quilt.

12 Thread the embroidery needle with three strands of floss. Sew straight lines of running stitches by hand to link the orbits into constellations. Make the running stitches large, about three per inch (2.5 cm).

13 Cut 1-inch (2.5 cm) binding strips crosswise from dark blue linen fabric. Bind the quilt, using a ¼-inch (6 mm) seam allowance and mitered corners.

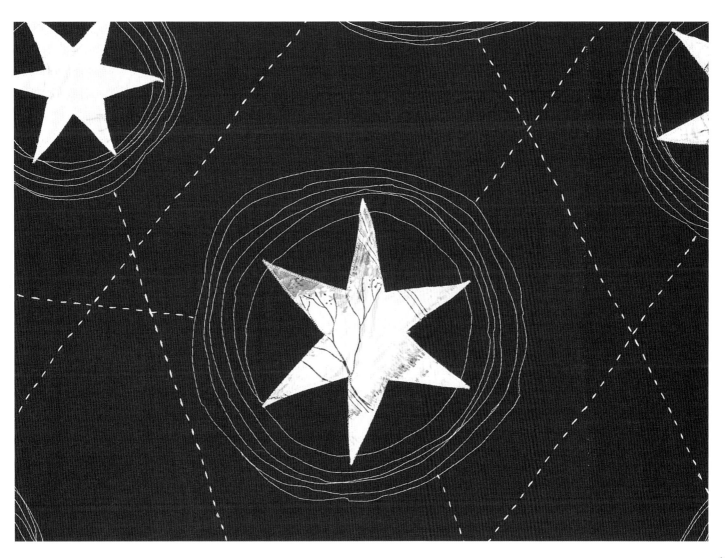

TWO TREES

CHRISTINA ROMEO

DESIGNER

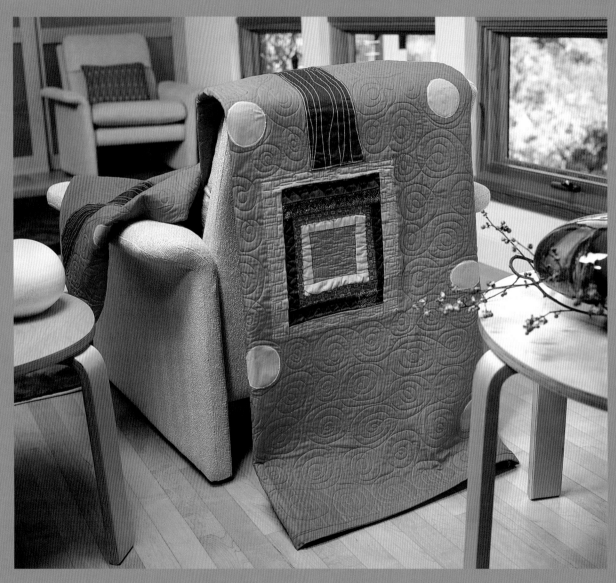

This inventive quilt uses several contemporary techniques including raw-edge appliqué, fusible appliqué, and relaxed strip piecing. Swirls of free-motion quilting create the illusion of a breeze rustling through the trees.

Finished size: approximately 77 x 56 inches (195.6 x 142.2 cm)

QUILT TOP AND BINDING:

4⅛ yards (3.8 m) of orange cotton fabric, 45 inches (114.3 cm) wide

BLOCKS:

Assorted pieces of light orange, dark orange print, brown, light blue, and tweed fabrics

APPLIQUÉS:

1½ yards (1.4 m) of dark brown cotton fabric, 45 inches (114.3 cm) wide

¼ yard (0.2 m) of bright blue cotton fabric, 45 inches (114.3 cm) wide

¾ yard (0.7 m) of paper-backed fusible web, 17 inches (43.2 cm) wide

BACKING:

4 yards (3.7 m) of light brown solid fabric, 45 inches (114.3 cm) wide

BATTING:

Low-loft cotton batting, 81 x 60 inches (205.7 x 152.4 cm)

THREAD:

Orange, brown, and blue sewing threads

TEMPLATES

See page 126

¼-inch (6 mm) seam allowance

INSTRUCTIONS

1 Cut two 5½ inch (14 cm) squares from orange cotton fabric for the centers of the tree blocks and reserve the remaining fabric for the quilt top. Cut the assorted pieces of light orange, dark orange print, dark brown, light blue, and tweed fabrics into 1½ inch (3.8 cm) strips for the tree blocks.

Figure 1

Figure 2

2 Piece each block by sewing a light blue strip with right sides together to the top and bottom edges of the orange center square. Trim the strip even with the edges of the square, and press the seams away from the center (see figure 1). In the same way, sew a light blue strip to the side edges of the center square (see figure 2). Continue sewing strips around the center of each block, finishing with light orange strips around the outside edges. As you complete sewing the strips of each color, trim the strips so the edges are straight but at a slight angle to give each block a relaxed look.

3 Use a rotary cutter, ruler, and mat to trim one tree block to 11½ inches (29.2 cm) square and the other to 12½ inches (31.8 cm) square.

4 Cut 3½-, 11½-, 12½-, and 15½-inch (8.9, 29.2, 31.8, and 39.4 cm) strips crosswise from orange cotton fabric in the lengths given (see figure 3) to piece together into rows for the quilt top. Sew the strips in each row together, and press the seams to one side.

5 Cut from dark brown fabric a trunk appliqué about 52½ x 4 inches (133.4 x 10.2 cm) for Row 2 and about 39 x 3 inches (99.1 x 7.6 cm) for Row 4 (see figure 3). Sew the trunks in place below the tree blocks as raw-edge appliqués. Adjust the sewing machine for straight stitching, threading the needle with dark brown thread and filling the bobbin with orange thread. Topstitch several wavy lines on each trunk appliqué. Thread the needle with white thread. Topstitch several more wavy lines on each trunk appliqué.

6 Stitch the five rows together to complete the quilt top. Press the seams to one side.

7 Trace Template A and Template B nine times each to make fusible appliqués from the bright blue fabric. Position the appliqués in three wavy rows on the quilt top. Fuse, following the manufacturer's directions. Thread the needle with white thread. Topstitch around the edge of each appliqué.

8 Cut eight 2-inch (5.1 cm) strips crosswise from the orange fabric and reserve for the binding. Cut the light brown fabric in half crosswise into two pieces measuring 64 inches (162.6 cm). Sew the halves together lengthwise to create the backing. Trim the backing to 82 x 61 inches (208.3 x 154.9 cm) with the seam centered.

9 Stack and baste the quilt layers.

10 Adjust the sewing machine for free-motion quilting. Thread the needle with orange thread and fill the bobbin with brown thread. Stitch a swirling design over the quilt top, and add quilting to the tree blocks as desired.

11 Bind the quilt, using a ½-inch (1.3 cm) seam allowance and butted corners.

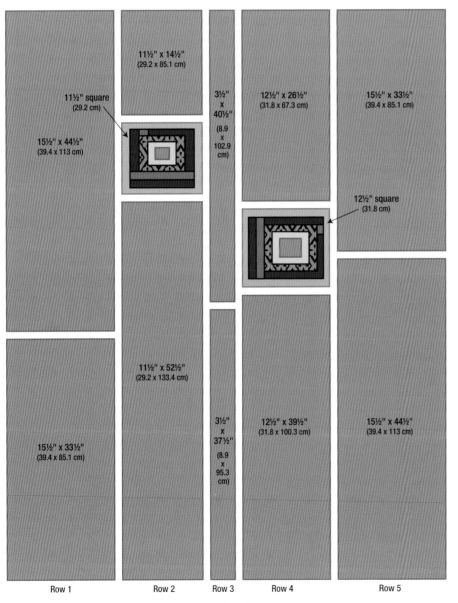

Row 1 | Row 2 | Row 3 | Row 4 | Row 5

11½" x 14½" (29.2 x 85.1 cm)

11½" square (29.2 cm)

15½" x 44½" (39.4 x 113 cm)

3½" x 40½" (8.9 x 102.9 cm)

12½" x 26½" (31.8 x 67.3 cm)

15½" x 33½" (39.4 x 85.1 cm)

12½" square (31.8 cm)

11½" x 52½" (29.2 x 133.4 cm)

15½" x 33½" (39.4 x 85.1 cm)

3½" x 37½" (8.9 x 95.3 cm)

12½" x 39½" (31.8 x 100.3 cm)

15½" x 44½" (39.4 x 113 cm)

Figure 3

LITTLE HILLS

AMY KAROL

DESIGNER

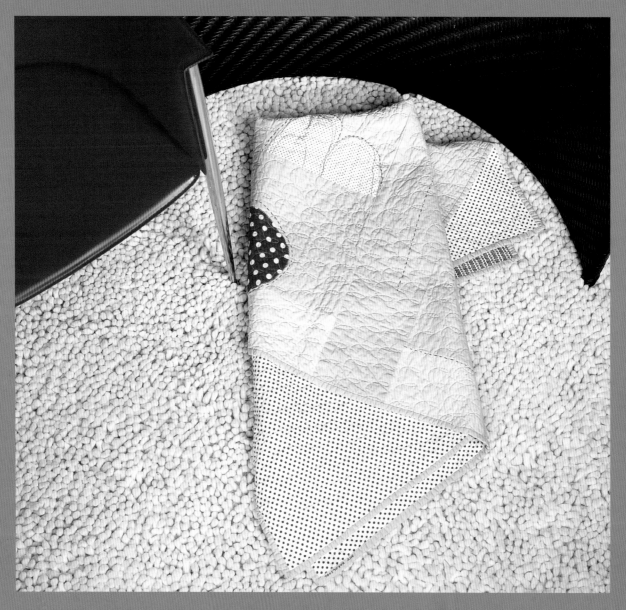

Create the imaginary landscape on this charming quilt with a combination of machine piecing and machine appliqué, and add amusing details with a touch of free-motion machine embroidery plus a few running stitches. To finish, quilt an allover design composed of row upon row of fanciful loops.

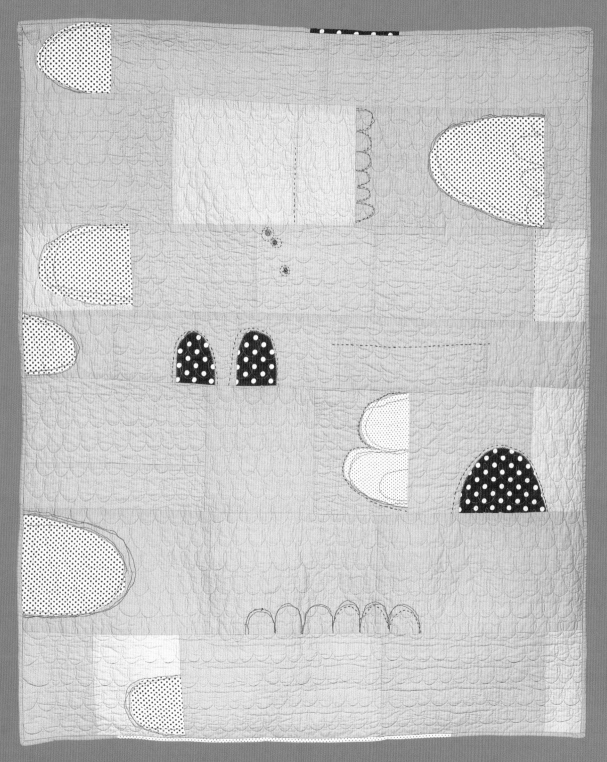

Finished size: approximately 59 x 49 inches (149.9 x 124.5 cm)

MATERIALS

BLOCKS:

½ yard (0.5 m) of solid lavender cotton fabric, 54 inches (137.2 cm) wide

2½ yards (2.3 m) of solid blue cotton fabric, 54 inches (137.2 cm) wide

APPLIQUÉS AND BACKING:

½ yard (0.5 m) of red cotton fabric with medium white polka dots for the hill appliqués, 54 inches (137.2 cm) wide

¼ yard (0.2 m) of white cotton fabric with tiny red polka dots for the hill appliqués, 54 inches (137.2 cm) wide

3 yards (2.7 m) of white cotton fabric with small red polka dots for the hill appliqués and backing, 54 inches (137.2 cm) wide

18 x 15½-inch (45.7 x 39.4 cm) piece of red/white print cotton fabric for the contrast accent on the backing

BATTING:

Low-loft cotton batting, 63 x 53 inches (160 x 134.6 cm)

THREAD, ETC:

Red, white, and blue sewing threads

Red embroidery floss

TOOLS & SUPPLIES

Embroidery needle with a large eye

¼-inch (6 mm) seam allowance

DESIGNER'S NOTE: To duplicate the soft look of this quilt, don't prewash the fabrics. When the completed quilt is laundered, the fabrics will pucker a little bit around the quilting stitches and create a gently worn appearance.

INSTRUCTIONS

1 Refer to figure 1 throughout. Cut the six accent blocks from lavender fabric. Cut the remaining blocks from blue fabric. Reserve the remaining blue fabric for binding strips.

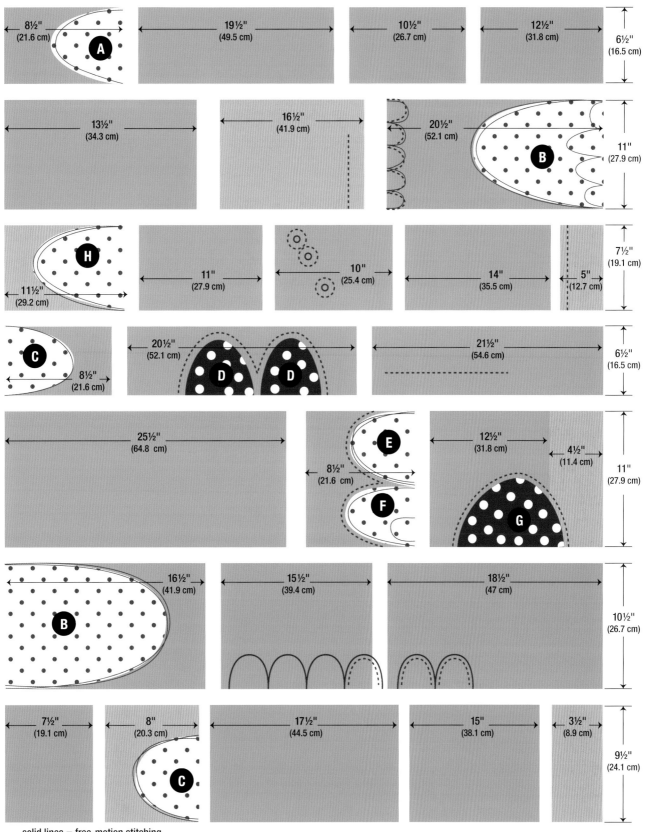

8½"
(21.6 cm)

A

19½"
(49.5 cm)

10½"
(26.7 cm)

12½"
(31.8 cm)

6½"
(16.5 cm)

13½"
(34.3 cm)

16½"
(41.9 cm)

20½"
(52.1 cm)

B

11"
(27.9 cm)

H

11½"
(29.2 cm)

11"
(27.9 cm)

10"
(25.4 cm)

14"
(35.5 cm)

5"
(12.7 cm)

7½"
(19.1 cm)

C

8½"
(21.6 cm)

20½"
(52.1 cm)

D   D

21½"
(54.6 cm)

6½"
(16.5 cm)

25½"
(64.8 cm)

E

8½"
(21.6 cm)

F

12½"
(31.8 cm)

4½"
(11.4 cm)

G

11"
(27.9 cm)

B

16½"
(41.9 cm)

15½"
(39.4 cm)

18½"
(47 cm)

10½"
(26.7 cm)

7½"
(19.1 cm)

8"
(20.3 cm)

C

17½"
(44.5 cm)

15"
(38.1 cm)

3½"
(8.9 cm)

9½"
(24.1 cm)

solid lines = free-motion stitching
broken lines = hand-embroidered running stitches

Figure 1

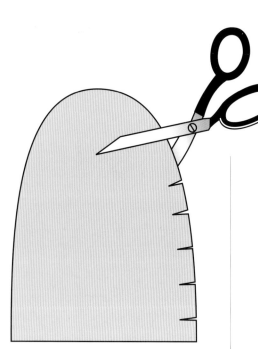

Figure 2

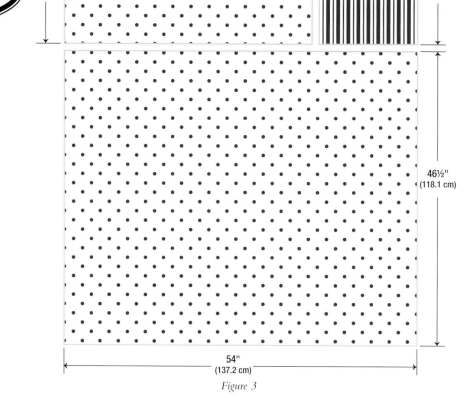

Figure 3

2 Cut out the following, using figure 1 to estimate the size and including an additional ¼ inch (6 mm) around each hill appliqué: from the white fabric with small white polka dots, one of A, two of B, two of C, and one of H; from the red fabric with medium white polka dots, two of D and one of G; from the white fabric with tiny white polka dots: one of E and one of F. Reserve the remaining fabrics for the binding strips and backing. Clip the seam allowance of each appliqué around the curved portion (see figure 2).

Fold the clipped seam allowance of each appliqué to the wrong side, and press.

3 Pin each appliqué in place on the corresponding blue or lavender block. Align the straight edge of each appliqué with the raw edge of the block.

4 Adjust the sewing machine for a narrow zigzag stitch, threading the needle and filling the bobbin with white thread. Stitch the curved portion of each appliqué.

5 Adjust the sewing machine for free-motion quilting, threading the needle and filling the bobbin with red thread. As desired, stitch the free-motion details as shown on the diagram.

6 Thread the embroidery needle with three strands of floss. As desired, sew running stitches to embellish selected details as shown on the diagram.

7 Adjust the sewing machine for a straight stitch, threading the needle and filling the bobbin with blue thread. Sew the blocks into seven rows, including the straight raw edges of the appliqués in the seams as you sew. Sew the rows together to complete the quilt top.

8 Cut the reserved white fabric with small red polka dots into two backing sections (see figure 3). Sew the smaller backing section to the contrast section and press the seams open. Sew this to the remaining backing section and press the seams open.

9 Stack and baste the quilt layers.

10 Adjust the sewing machine for free-motion quilting, threading the needle with blue thread and filling the bobbin with white thread. Stitch rows of loops over the entire quilt.

11 Cut 1-inch (2.5 cm) crosswise strips from the reserved blue and polka dot fabrics. Bind the quilt, using a ¼-inch (6 mm) seam allowance and mitered corners.

BOLD CHINTZ

NIKI BONNETT

DESIGNER

This lively quilt combines pieced blocks with blocks cut from whole cloth. All the blocks are irregular and asymmetrical by design, so enjoy taking a relaxed approach when constructing them.

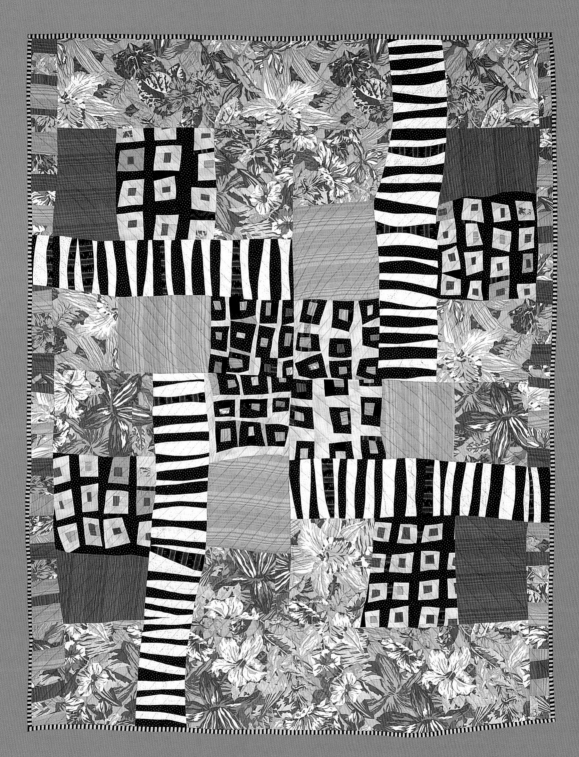

Finished size: approximately 80 x 64 inches (203.2 x 162.6 cm)

MATERIALS

BLOCKS:

2 yards (1.4 m) of dark charcoal tone-on-tone print cotton fabric, 54 inches (137.2 cm) wide

1 yard each (0.9 m) of light gray and off-white tone-on-tone print cotton fabrics, 54 inches (137.2 cm) wide

1 yard (0.9 m) each of yellow and orange tone-on-tone striped print cotton fabrics, 54 inches (137.2 cm) wide

1½ yards (1.4 m) of floral print chintz fabric, 52 inches (132.1 cm) wide

BACKING:

4 yards (3.7 m) of floral print chintz fabric, 52 inches (132.1 cm) wide

BATTING:

Low-loft batting, 85 x 68 inches (215.9 x 172.7 cm)

BINDING:

½ yard (0.5 m) of yellow/charcoal striped cotton fabric, 54 inches (137.2 cm) wide

THREAD:

Gray, orange, and purple sewing threads

TOOLS

Fabric chalk marker

¼-inch (6 mm) seam allowance

INSTRUCTIONS

1 Prewash all fabrics.

2 Cut eight 30 x 9-inch (76.2 x 22.9 cm) pieces each from charcoal and from off-white fabric. Stack a charcoal and an off-white piece with right sides facing up (see figure 1) to make eight pairs.

3 Use a rotary cutter to slice the stacked fabrics into at least 18 irregular strips from about 1 to 1¾ inches (2.5 to 4.4 cm) wide (see figure 2). Lift up each strip from the top layer of fabric and place it next to the corresponding strip from the layer underneath (see figure 3). Switch every other strip to make eight sets of 18 alternating charcoal and off-white strips to piece into rows (see figure 4).

4 Adjust the sewing machine for straight stitching, threading the needle and filling the bobbin with gray thread. Lay the first strip from one set right side up. Lay the second strip from this set right side down, aligning the raw edges; pin

DESIGNER'S NOTE: Big, colorful prints are essential for this quilt. Cotton chintz, customarily selected for home decorating projects such as draperies and slipcovers, will have the large-scale floral motifs you need for some of the blocks and the backing; it's a good idea to select the chintz prints first, and choose the remaining fabrics to harmonize. You'll need to prewash the chintz fabrics to remove their sheen and stiff finish and make them more compatible with the other fabrics.

To simplify the construction of this quilt, you could substitute striped and geometric print fabrics for the pieced blocks. However, much of the visual excitement of this quilt comes from the asymmetry and irregularity of the different design elements. You can randomly introduce coordinating fabric scraps into some of the blocks, creating further interest.

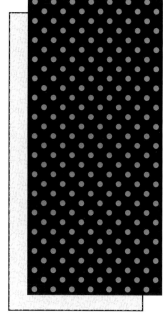

Figure 1

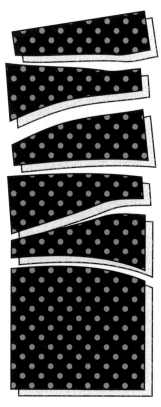

Figure 2

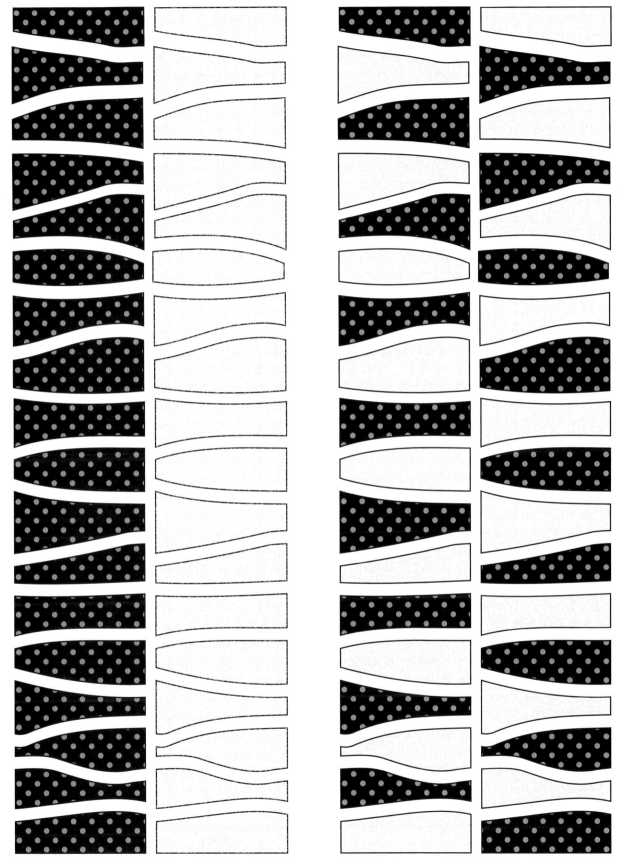

Figure 3

Figure 4

the pieces together, even though the fabric strip on top may not lie flat (see figure 5). Stitch the seam, easing the edges together and pausing as needed with the needle down in the fabrics to align the pieces. In this way, stitch each set of strips into rows.

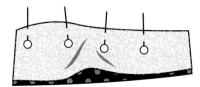

Figure 5

5 Make four "A" blocks from the pieced rows. To make each "A" block, stitch together two pieced rows so the charcoal and off-white strips alternate (see figure 6). Press the seams to one side, clipping the seam allowances where needed so they lie flat. Trim two of the "A" blocks so they are 40¼ inches (102.2 cm) long, and trim two "A" blocks so they are 32¼ inches (81.9 cm) long.

6 Use a rotary cutter and the orange and yellow fabrics to cut 112 four-sided pieces about 1 to 1¾ nches (2.5 to 4.4 cm) square. These pieces should be irregular in shape and do not require right-angle corners (see figure 7).

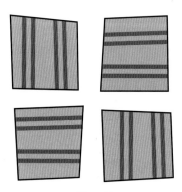

Figure 7

seam

Figure 6 - A Block

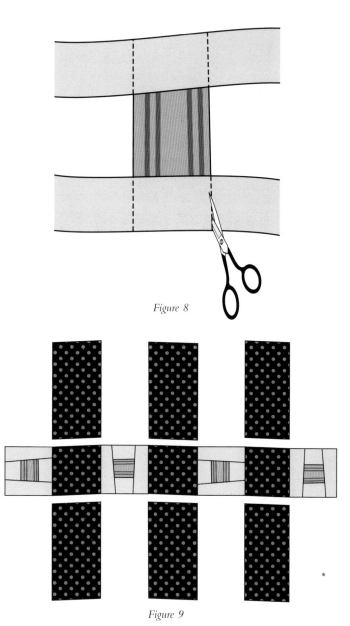

Figure 8

Figure 9

7 Use a rotary cutter to cut several crosswise strips from the gray and charcoal fabrics in various widths from about ¾ to 1¾ inches (1.9 to 4.4 cm). Stitch a gray strip to the top and bottom edges of an orange or yellow piece, press the seams toward the gray strips, and trim the gray strips even with the edge of the orange or yellow piece (see figure 8); save the gray trimmings. Sew a gray strip to each side edge in the same way. Repeat to make a total of 64 sections with gray borders, using the long uncut strips as well as the trimmings to make the borders. Sew charcoal strips around the remaining 48 yellow and orange pieces in the same way. Cut additional crosswise strips as necessary to complete all 112 bordered sections.

Figure 10 - B Block

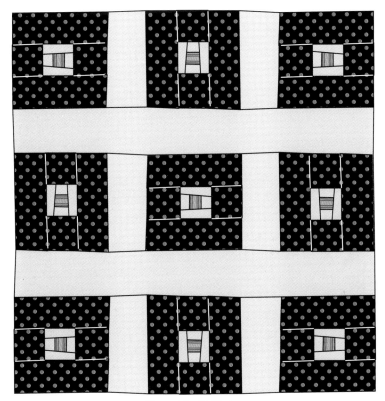

Figure 11 - C Block

8 Use a rotary cutter to cut several crosswise strips from the charcoal and gray fabrics in various widths from about 1 to 2 inches (2.5 to 5.1 cm). Join four of the gray-bordered sections by sewing a charcoal strip in between to make each of 16 rows, trimming the charcoal strip as needed (see figure 9). Use the trimmings as in step 7 where possible. Join four of the rows together with a charcoal strip in between to make four "B" blocks (see figure 10). Complete each "B" block by sewing a charcoal strip to each edge. In the same way, join three of the charcoal-bordered sections together with a gray strip in between to make 12 rows, then join three rows together to make four "C" blocks (see figure 11). Complete each "C" block by sewing a gray strip to each edge. Cut additional crosswise strips as necessary to complete the blocks.

9 Cut about 25 strips approximately 2 to 2½ x 4 inches (5.1 to 6.4 x 10.2 cm) each from the chintz, the orange tone-on-tone stripe, and the yellow tone-on-tone stripe fabrics. Sew the strips, alternating the colors, into one long strip to make a filler strip 4 inches (10.2 cm) wide.

10 Refer to figure 12 as a guide for cutting and piecing the blocks for each of the four main sections for the quilt top. Note that two of these four main sections follow one design, while the other two follow another. Although the two designs have common elements, the proportions of the elements are different due to the orientation of the blocks. Each main section should be created to fit the length of the "A" blocks you made in step 5; the sections with the longer "A" blocks will be oriented vertically, while the remaining two sections will be oriented horizontally. Begin making each main section by using an "A" block as the center row. Place a "C" block in the bottom row. Place a "B" block in the top row. Fill the spaces remaining in the rows with square and rectangular blocks cut from the chintz fabric and the yellow and orange tone-on-tone striped prints; vary the fabrics used for these blocks among the four sections for visual interest.

11 Sew the blocks in each row together. To make any irregular edges fit together, fold under the seam allowance along one edge ¼ inch (6 mm), lay this over the adjoining edge, and mark the seamline with chalk (see figure 13). Trim the adjoining edge ¼ inch (6 mm) from the chalk-marked line to leave a seam allowance. Sew the two edges together. Repeat as needed to complete each main section; note that you may be trimming away some of the "B" and "C" blocks to fit your design.

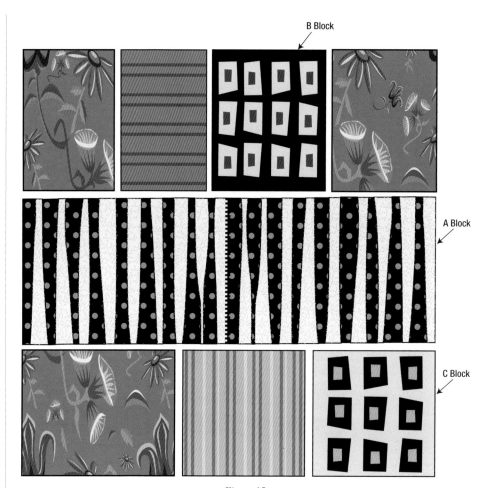

Figure 12

12 Arrange the four main sections for the quilt top so all the corner "C" blocks meet in the center (see figure 14). Measure each of the four sections for the quilt top. Insert pieces of filler strip or additional strips of chintz if necessary along the outside edges so each of the four sections measures 40

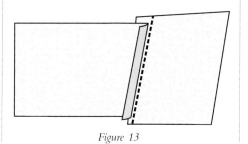

Figure 13

¼ x 32¼ inches (102.2 x 81.9 cm). Sew the top two sections together. Sew the bottom two sections together. Sew these sections together to complete the quilt top.

13 Cut the backing fabric crosswise into two pieces, each 2 yards (1.8 m) long. Sew them together with a lengthwise seam. Trim the backing to 86 x 69 inches (218.4 x 175.3 cm) with the seam in the center. Or, as an option, you can piece together fabrics left over from the quilt top with the chintz backing fabric to create a second design and make the quilt reversible.

14 Stack and baste the quilt layers.

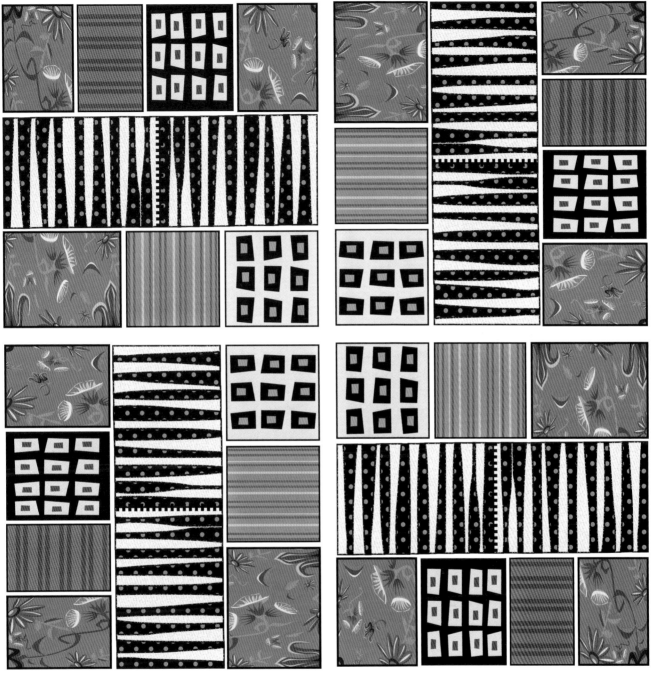

Figure 14

15 Adjust the sewing machine for straight-stitch quilting. Thread the needle with orange thread and fill the bobbin with purple thread. Quilt parallel rows of Vs spaced from 1 to 1½ inches (2.5 to 3.8 cm) apart, with the point of the V near the center of the quilt.

16 Cut the charcoal/yellow striped fabric crosswise into 2-inch (5.1 cm) binding strips. Bind the quilt, using a ½-inch (1.3 cm) seam allowance and butted corners.

Sparrow (page 28)

enlarge 300%

TUMBLING LEAVES (PAGE 44)

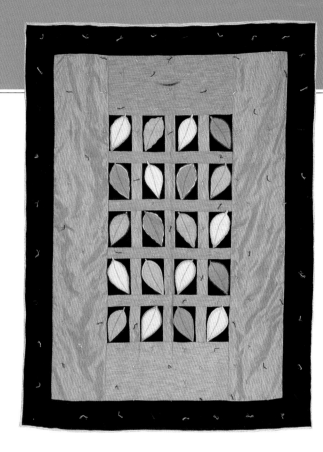

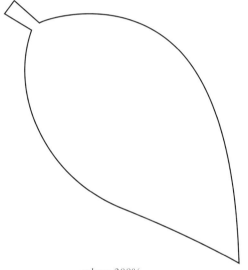

enlarge 200%

TEMPLATE A

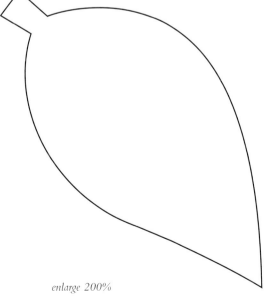

enlarge 200%

TEMPLATE B

EASY CHENILLE (PAGE 48)

enlarge 200%

TEMPLATE A

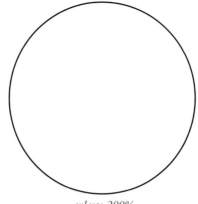

enlarge 200%

TEMPLATE B

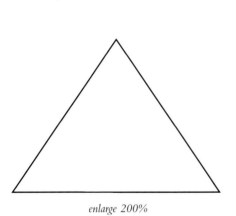

enlarge 200%

TEMPLATE C

FLOWERS (PAGE 82)

enlarge 200%

TEMPLATE A

enlarge 200%

TEMPLATE B

Sea Moods (page 90)

templates actual size

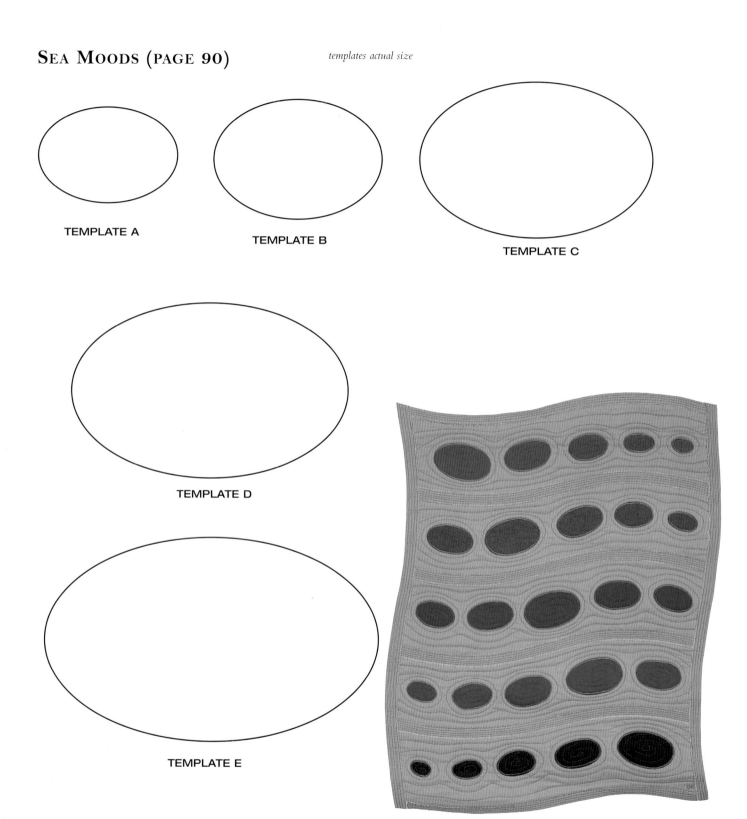

TEMPLATE A

TEMPLATE B

TEMPLATE C

TEMPLATE D

TEMPLATE E

CONSTELLATIONS (PAGE 98)

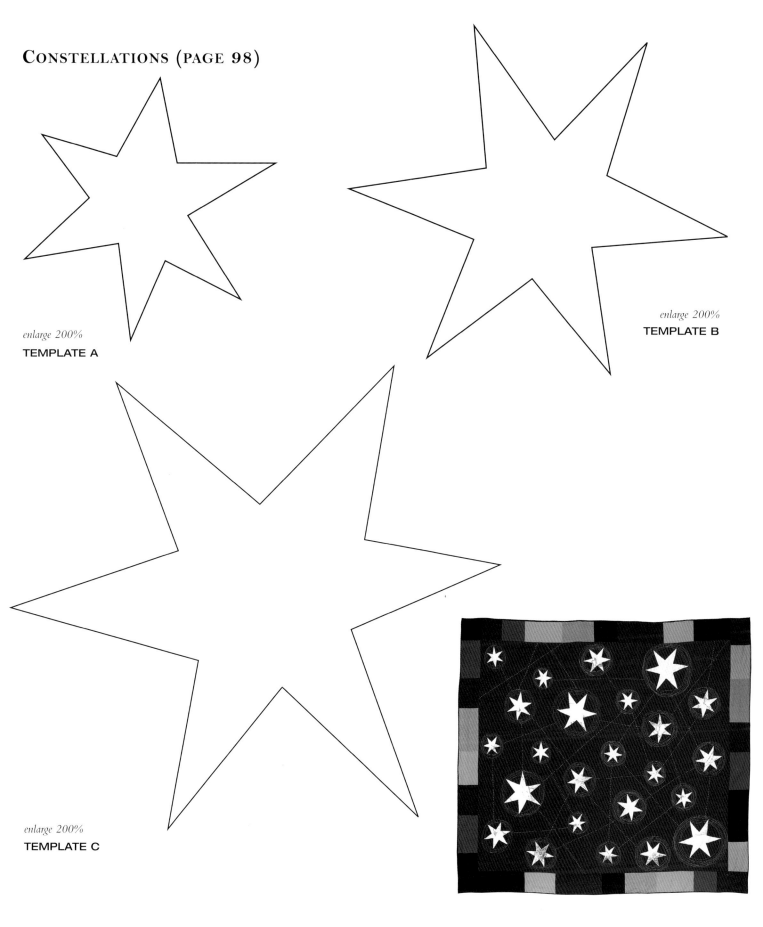

enlarge 200%

TEMPLATE A

enlarge 200%

TEMPLATE B

enlarge 200%

TEMPLATE C

Two Trees (page 102)

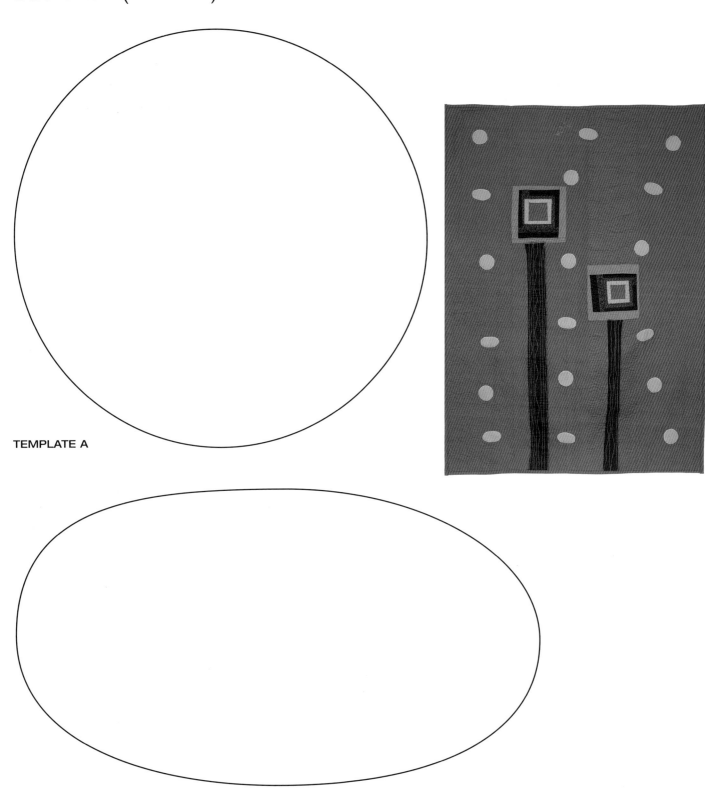

TEMPLATE A

TEMPLATE B

ABOUT THE DESIGNERS

Niki Bonnett holds a B.F.A. from the Rhode Island School of Design. After a long career in graphic design, she became a full-time artist in 1993. Her work has been exhibited at Quilt National, Craft USA, Wesserling Textile Museum (France), Palais Rastede (Germany), and The American Craft Museum (now the Museum of Arts and Design). Niki has been featured in *Fiberarts* and *Art/Quilt* magazines, in *The Art Quilt* by Robert Shaw (Beaux Arts Editions, 1997) and in *Creative Collage for Crafters* (Lark Books, 2002). She teaches and lectures nationally and is a member of the Southern Highland Craft Guild. Visit www.NikiB.com for more information on her work.

Rachel Fields has sewn since taking a home economics class in high school, but has concentrated on making clothes. She's excited about applying her sewing skills to her first quilt, made for this book. A native of Asheville, North Carolina, Rachel recently graduated from college with a degree in art history. She's currently exploring her career options by working at several internships.

Dianne Firth made her first traditional quilt for a bed in the early 1980s. Many of her works are informed by her observations of the environment and her training as a landscape architect. Dianne currently heads the Landscape Architecture Department at the University of Canberra, Australia. She is recognized in Australia and internationally through her works in major exhibitions and in public and private collections.

Xavora Fisher was born in Suriname, South America, and started Xaboke Organics in 2002. A self-taught quilter and designer of children's boutique wear, she creates each piece with individuality and comfort in mind. Because she primarily uses organic cotton fabric, her designs appeal to individuals with sensitive skin. Visit www.Xabokeorganics.com to find out more about her work.

Wendi Gratz skipped home economics in favor of wood and metal shop, so she didn't learn to use a sewing machine until college. Her first project was a badly made tablecloth; her second was designing and making all the costumes for a play. She now makes dolls, clothes, and quilts. Initially attracted by the lovely, dense texture of antique quilts, she discovered that she didn't like the fussy cutting and piecing required to make them. Her own quilts have the feel of those antiques, but with more contemporary design and simple construction. Wendi lives in Atlanta, Georgia, with her family and her sewing machine.

Amy Karol started sewing at age three; upon high school graduation she received her own sewing machine, the same one she uses today. Amy received a degree in interior architecture from the University of Oregon in 1996, with a minor in costume construction. Her quilts show around the United States in various shops and galleries. More than 20 pieces are in a permanent collection in Japan. Amy's blog, Angry Chicken, was a finalist for the 2006 Bloggie award for best craft blog. She has contributed to several craft books slated for release in 2007, including one of her own. Amy also enjoys making music, gardening, cooking, and raising her two daughters with her husband. She can be contacted at amy@kingpod.com.

The sewing machine was a fixture in **Hillary Lang's** life after a home economics class in middle school. Hillary later spent any free moments between her various careers (librarian, programmer, online vintage shop owner) working on sewing and craft projects. Now, as a stay-at-home mom, she's able to fully dedicate herself to sewing and designing. Her work is strongly influenced by children's book illustration and vintage toys. On her website www.weewonderfuls.com, Hillary blogs about kids, crafts, and finding inspiration. In addition, she contributes projects to magazines and books, and designs her own line of toys and patterns.

Shari Lidji lives in Dallas, Texas, where she works out of her Red Llama Studio. Inspired by family and a job as a graphic designer, she brings her love of art and color to each quilt. Shari is thrilled to create something that people truly treasure.

Joan K. Morris's artistic endeavors have led her down many successful creative paths, including costume design for motion pictures and ceramics. Joan has contributed projects for numerous Lark books, including *Beautiful Ribbon Crafts* (2003), *Gifts For Baby* (2004), *Creating Fantastic Vases* (2003), *Hardware Style* (2004), and *Hip Handbags* (2005).

Christina Romeo is a multimedia artist with a strong pull toward textile design. As a child, she learned to cross-stitch, collage, and reconstruct clothes into abstract creations. After a 10-year career in the dental health profession, Christina now pursues art full time, selling work throughout Canada and the United States and from her website. Her studio is located in the heart of the Selkirk Mountains, in Revelstoke, British Columbia. For more information on her work, visit www.jamtartbaby.com.

Jude Stuecker made her first quilt for a design project in high school. Fourteen years later, she's still hooked. She works from a studio in her home in Asheville, North Carolina. Her designs can be found at galleries and in her traveling tent at craft shows throughout the southeastern United States.

Jen Swearington is the creator of Jennythreads, hand-dyed silk clothing and accessories. Her contemporary mixed-media quilts are exhibited nationally, and have been featured on the cover of *Fiberarts* magazine and in *Surface Design Journal*. Her work has also appeared in *Altered Art* (2004), *Exquisite Embellishments for Your Clothes* (2006), and *Altered Objects* (2006), all published by Lark Books. Visit www.jennythreads.net to see more of her work.

Karen James Swing has loved working with anything fiber her whole life, and has made art quilts for nearly 20 years. She particularly enjoys using large print fabrics, cutting them up to "re-invent" the pattern. Karen lives and works in the mountains of North Carolina, which are a constant source of inspiration.

INDEX

Appliqué, 20–21
Art quilts, 16
Assembling, 22
Backings, 11
Basting, 13, 23
Basting spray, 15
Batting, 11–12
Beds, measuring, 15
Binding, 23–25
    Double-layer, 25
Borders, attaching, 22
Care requirements, for fabrics, 11
Corners
    Butted, 25
    Mitered, 23–24
Cutting, 13–14
Darning foot, 12, 19
Fabrics, choosing, 11
Freezer paper, 14
Fusible web, 14
Glue sticks, 15
Hand-sewing techniques, 21
Hand tying, 12, 21
Hanging sleeves, 16
Marking, 15
Needles
    Hand-sewing, 12
    Machine, 17
Pressing, 14, 17
Prewashing, 11, 108, 114
Quilt bar attachment, 18
Quilting
    Echo, 19
    Free-motion, 19
    Outline, 19
    Stitch in the ditch, 18
    Straight-stitch, 17
Running stitch, 21
Sashing strips, adding, 22
Scale, 10
Seams, 17
Sewing machines, 12–13
Shrinkage, 11
Signatures, 11
Sizes of quilts, standard, 15
Stacking, 22
Substituting fabrics, 11
Thread, 13
Tops, 11
Tying, 21
Walking foot, 12, 18

ACKNOWLEDGMENTS

This book wouldn't have been possible with the creativity of the talented fiber artists who designed and made quilts especially for this book. Their artistry is evident throughout. Please take a moment to read the biographies of these special women.

Senior editor Suzanne J.E. Tourtillott and associate editor Nathalie Mornu spent lots of time with the designers to develop the gorgeous projects, and Peggy Bendel's skill as a technical editor made the text accurate and easy to read. Art director Dana Irwin conceived a beautiful design, and photographer Stewart O'Shields captured on film the personality of each individual quilt. Illustrator Orrin Lundgren painstakingly crafted all the quiltmaking imagery.

Public Interest Properties, Inc., and Mobilia, both in downtown Asheville, N.C., allowed us to use their facilities for the photo shoot, and homeowners Grant and Terri Todd opened their lovely home for our use.

My thanks to all for helping produce *Simple Contemporary Quilts*.